# What To Do
# When People Get on Your Nerves!

A Spiritual Guide with Practical Solutions for Dealing with the
Obnoxious, Aggravating, **CRAZY**...things people say and do

Written By MoriEl Randolph        Illustrations By Mark Hill

● *FreshView Publishing* ●

Published by FreshView Publishing

Clinton, MD 20735
(301) 856-8051

ISBN 978-1-60402-724-2
ISBN 978-0-6151-5960-7

First published by FreshView Publishing December 28, 2007

Printed in the United States of America
Winfield, Kansas

Set in Book Antiqua
Book Design by Daniel Middleton
www.scribefreelance.com

ISBN 978-0-6151-5960-7

9 780615 159607

# Acknowledgements

Writing this guide and seeing it published became a very fervent dream of mine. However, it would have never become a reality had it not been for my amazing husband. From the beginning, my life has been enriched by this wonderful man as THE ALMIGHTY continues to use him in ways that I would have never imagined.

I give all the praise to My FATHER in Heaven for my husband who has been a true hero, my knight in shinning armor. Thank you honey, for believing in me and not giving up on my dream.

I would also like to acknowledge my editors Liz Lounsbury and Kenneth Broadway for their professionalism and inspiring input, along with Daniel Middleton and illustrator, Mark Hill for their contributions to the book's design and presentation. I am also thankful for the concepts and aspirations that make FreshView Books & Seminars the perfect vehicle through which I share this guide and its principles with the world.

# The Buzz About
# What To Do When People Get on Your Nerves

"Reading and applying the principles of *What To Do When People Get on Your Nerves* will improve your self-esteem, enhance your communication skills and empower you to have a happier life."

Eunice Lindenwhite
Executive Director, Community Services
Coalition and Certified Facilitator of Compassion Power Program

"Great Book! *What To Do When People Get on Your Nerves* is a fresh, introspective look at how best to grow, love and be at peace in a chaotic world."

Charlene Taylor
President and CEO
Institute for Black Charities
www.blackcharities.net

"Another self help, manage your coworkers, keep a cool head book, I thought. **Not so, not so at all**. MoriEl Randolph gives you a fresh way of looking at your "offenders," and your response to them. She guides you through your feelings and, more importantly, where they come from and how they govern behavior.

"This book should be required reading for anyone who has felt a rise in blood pressure, cussed, cried or became upset when someone got on their nerves. That would be all of us."

Esther Williams
Recording Artist/Actress
Washington Jazz Arts Institute Board Officer
www.dcjazzmusic.org

# The Buzz Continues

*"What To Do When People Get on Your Nerves* does a great job of informing readers how one can handle the challenges of the workplace, at home and in personal relationships. Her practical tips on handling people who get on your nerves make this an interesting read for any person who wants to become a better person."

Tracey Webb
Founder
Black Benefactors
blackbenefactors.org

*"What To Do When People Get on Your Nerves* offers the best of all worlds; the advice of a counselor combined with the love of a close friend tapered with spiritual insight.

"Finally a book that offers help for the whole person--mentally and spiritually."

Kepa Freeman
Executive Director
TeensExpress
www.teensexpress.org

"This book is an inspirational tool that has helped me self examine myself and my everyday situations. I encourage anyone who is looking for insight on how to handle people who get on your nerves to read this awesome book."

Marquita Barksdale
Educator
Calvary Christian Academy

*What To Do When People Get on Your Nerves* "is not only food for the spirit, it is also food for thought." "It teaches us "Caring Concern.""

Patricia Conway
Grants Management Specialist
Efforts, Inc.

# | Contents

# Dedication

This Book is dedicated to
**PORTIA-SERENA**
It was she who taught me how to develop true Caring Concern
for others.

For over 30 years she stood by me as my
Pastor
Teacher
Mentor
Sister in the belief
and Best Friend
I will cherish her always as a precious gift given to me by
my FATHER in Heaven through HIS Holy Son.

The life she lived was a true witness of HIS ALMIGHTY Power.

# Who Should Read This Book

The style of writing for this guide is of an idiosyncratic nature, in other words its jargon and content is extremely simple and its approach very unconventional. So, if you are of the academia but feel you may benefit from the content of this book, then simply remove your scholastic hat, take your shoes off and relax. It should be fun, as I am certain that you will find the experience quite refreshing.

I am equally certain that anyone drawn by the title of this book is probably a lot like me, not the most patient individual in the world. You may be one who is too easily annoyed by the thoughtless or ridiculous things people say or do — or how they sit around and complain afterwards, blaming everyone but themselves for the consequences.

If this describes you, then this book could be of great value to you.

On the other hand, if you're thinking it will tell you how to control those who can kindle such vexation, I'm afraid this guide will not be of much help to you.

Although, purchasing a ticket to another planet may, one day, be an option, since here on planet Earth it simply doesn't work that way.

By now you may be thinking: "Is this another one of those self-help books?"

Well duhhh-yeah.

And, though the idea of sending all the irritating people in our lives to another planet is a tempting concept to consider, this is not fiction.  In fact, this may turn out to be one of the strongest doses of reality you've had in a long time.

This book is about exercising your power over the one and only entity you can control.  That entity would be YOU.

It's about the peace of mind that comes with living life as stress free as is humanly possible, in spite of the irritating people you may encounter.

Now when it comes to the subject of peace, there is one entity, I believe, that cannot be overlooked.  HE is the author of peace.  I refer to HIM as my heavenly FATHER or by a title only HE is worthy of: THE ALMIGHTY.

So, although this is not a religious book (i.e., based on any denominational doctrine) I will be referring to HIS WORD when necessary.  In fact, each chapter ends with an excerpt from what has been preserved of HIS written word.

Hence, if you believe in a power greater than yourself and have a longing to live life to the fullest, free from the unnecessary stress generated by this crazy world we live in, then you are in for a treat.

If you are a non-believer, or if your belief system is not centered around The Christ, but you have no difficulty reading material written by those who do believe, I feel confident that you too will find the principles and light shed in this guide stimulating, practical and simple to apply.

# Introduction

I contacted a client during business hours, which was normal. However, this time, unlike others, her response was cold. After my usual greeting, to which I would normally receive a warm reception, she simply asked me how she could help me.

I asked if she was having a bad day. She instantly apologized for her tone and shared how much the supervisor and co-workers were getting on her nerves.

She went on to share the frustration she experienced as she endeavored to gather all the necessary figures and documents requested by her supervisor, while watching the supervisor and coworkers sitting around doing virtually nothing.

She had become weary and resentful as she considered the possibility of having to work overtime in order to get every-thing done — overtime for which she would not get paid.

I understood exactly how she felt and pointed out that she had choices to make. If her supervisor was truly acting this way, it was only because she could. In other words, people treat us the way we teach them to. My client had allowed this type of treatment from her supervisor for far too long; pro-testing now could possibly place her job at risk. Therefore, having no control over her supervisor or co-workers, she need-ed to determine what she could control.

After giving some thought to what I shared with her, she stopped focusing on others and looked to the control she had over her own actions.

Immediately, she realized by simply coming in early, before the others, she could be more productive. Though she would still put in overtime, she would have a less stressful day and was assured of no distractions. Since she needed her job and (at that time) was in no position to put it in jeopardy, she could live with the overtime without pay if she could at least get home on time.

On the other hand, she could have decided that coming in earlier or staying late was just unacceptable. That determination would have caused her stress level to escalate along with her workload. Consequently, she would have inevitably done or said something that would have jeopardized her job, not to mention her health.

This example demonstrates how sometimes we must accept the circumstances within our lives, at least on a temporary basis. But, while doing so, we must be careful to make wise choices for our own sakes. For it will be our choices that will enable us to deal with our temporary circumstances in the most comfortable or expeditious way possible, while mapping out a plan for change.

In other words, there will always be circumstances we cannot control. So instead of resenting that fact (which won't change), we can focus on what we can control and what we can change.

This guide will help.

But what about the people? All those **CRAZY** folks we have to deal with!

Wouldn't it be wonderful if, regardless of how obnoxious, moody or dysfunctional individuals may behave, you could live your life without being negatively affected by them?

Wouldn't it be great if, regardless of your profession, family or relationships, you could live your life free of unnecessary stress—the type of stress that comes with having to deal with the drama and changes people go through?

Do you work with the public? How terrific would it be to help or assist any knucklehead in the country without having your cool disrupted?

Well, it's not possible to have absolutely no feelings evoked or provoked as a result of annoying things people may do, not if you live in a human body. But, it is possible to prevent those feelings from taking a toll on your body.

Most importantly, it is absolutely POSSIBLE to keep other people from having a negative effect on your life.

Now, I feel I must interject again that this book is based on the principles, wisdom and WORD of THE ALMIGHTY through HIS Son. The source of power needed to fully and successfully apply all of its principles comes from the same source that enables us all to move and breathe and have our being.

With that said, please keep in mind that this guide is not just for believers or professed Christians. It will shed refreshing light, insight and understanding to all its readers.

So let's explore **What You Can Do When People Get On Your *NERVES*.**

*When wisdom guides your actions, when beneficial knowledge is pleasant to you, then your decisions shall preserve you, and under-standing shall keep you...*

# Chapter 1

Life is a B . . . eautiful Thing.
It's People Who Can Act
Like B . . . easts!

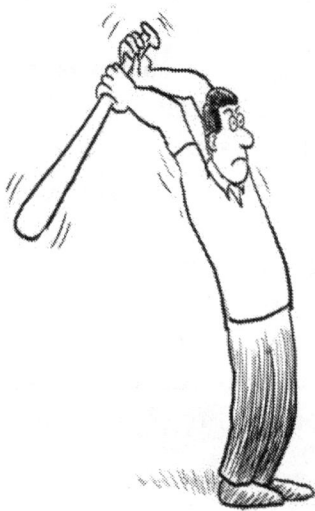

IT'S TRUE YOU know. I wish to address this topic because I think it is absolutely terrible the way Life receives such a bum rap for the things that occur.

Life is a good thing. It must be, because without it we would all be dead—or at least our bodies would be. In other words, without Life, humans would be able to participate in **no-thing**.

The bad, unfortunate, evil or sad things that occur while we're experiencing this beautiful thing we call Life have nothing to do with Life itself.

It's like the air we breathe. Air is good, but if humans make choices that pollute the air or if one human should place a substance within it that would kill the bodies of others, do we blame the air? Of course not...well, maybe there are those who would.

But assuming that everyone reading this book is not nutty, let's just go with NO as the answer to that question.

If not for the existence or composition of air, many things could not occur. For example, the spread of certain diseases, viruses, radiation, oh and what's that other thing? Oh yeah—*Life*!

In other words, regardless of what humans may do to the air or put in it, we don't get mad at it or call it names. We like the air; we need the air.

So why then do we blame Life for so much? We call it names. Some claim to hate it. We say things like "Well that's Life for ya," "Life's not fair" or "Life sucks."

One of the reasons so many wish to blame Life for their troubles or problems is because it's the perfect scapegoat. It never gets an attitude or talks back, and it's always available, at least as long as you are.

But it needn't feel bad; for if they didn't blame Life, they would find something or someone else to blame.

One of the greatest problems or challenges we face as human beings is taking responsibility for our own actions, choices or decisions.   Since the beginning of time humans have been inclined to blame the other guy or woman or something.

It's certainly true that throughout childhood and adolescence, our lives can be greatly affected by the choices and decisions of others.   However, as adults, the majority of the negative things that occur in our lives are due to our own choices and decisions.

But what never ceases to amaze me is the extent or extreme that we go through to keep from accepting the challenge of responsibility.  Though I understand the reasons why, it amazes me still.

You see, no matter who goes or comes, no matter who lives or dies, as long as you are in your body, you will have one person on the planet who will always be with you. One person you cannot dismiss or put out of your life. One person, like it or not, you must live with 24/7.  That one person is you.

For many, the choices they've made or things they've done make it hard for them to live with themselves.

So in order to make existence as bearable as possible, they do whatever it takes to feel good about who they are.

When people find it too difficult to accept their choices, they seek ways of escape from themselves via drugs, food, sex, work, etc.

Our need to think positively about ourselves also explains why we often go to such extremes to look good, at least in the eyes of those outside of ourselves. This need for self-approval is so strong that we often deny the truth. Moreover, we avoid taking responsibility for our actions to the point where we frequently blame our actions on something or someone else.

But believe me, it's a futile and powerless path. Moreover, Life does not have to be this way. In fact, one can only experience the fullness of what Life has to offer when one finds the courage to accept oneself as one is (bad choices and all). Of course, you must be willing to put forth the effort to work on what needs fixing.

For the truth is, we all have things that need fixing.

Yes, Life is wonderful. It's not even hard. It's not hard to live. All you have to do is wake up each day and there you are, you're living.

What's hard is dealing with the consequences brought about by the choices made by our government, leaders, teachers, parents, children, spouse (past or present) and, most importantly, ourselves.

Life is good, for with each new day comes the possibility of making it better no matter how good it already is or how bad.

As for freedom from people who get on your nerves, the first step is taking responsibility for the person you are. Taking this step is the only way the process can begin, and you must take it regardless of the mistakes you've made or the people you've hurt.

Why? Because then, and only then, can we become aware of our own faults and shortcomings. Once this occurs, the issues or hang-ups of others won't matter as much.

It will become easier to overlook their quirks, whatever they may be.

You will gain the ability to live your life according to the truth regarding yourself and the choices you've made. This ability alone will make you an exceptional human being because most people **do not** admit to themselves who they truly are.

So regardless of how well people may manage to hide what they really think of themselves, the truth is:

**We cannot grow on lies, nor can we fight or change what we don't or won't acknowledge.**

*Guard your thoughts with all diligence;*
*for in them are issues of life*

# NOTES

# Chapter 2

## When People Get On Your Nerves In General

HOW MANY TIMES have you found yourself murmuring the title of this book or a similar thought such as "People are a TRIP!"

It seems more than ever people have so many issues, hangups, problems and mood swings. You just don't know what to expect.

When someone new comes into your life, either via a personal relationship or a job, you sometimes find yourself dreading what you will discover or what kind of experience, hurt or disappointment you may encounter.

The fact that people, in general, come with varied amounts of baggage is not going to change.

From the day we make our entrance into this world, our lives are affected, and many times marred, by the experiences we encounter with other human beings.

Believe it or not, the problem isn't the baggage we all acquire. The problem is a growing disinterest in what can cause baggage to build up in the first place. We rarely look at the cause of a matter, especially when it comes to whatever may be the matter with another human being.

Appreciation for human life has taken a great decline, and Caring Concern for one another — What's that?

Though it's sad, we accept that there are times when we might not receive a glance or smile from someone on the street or even in our own homes for that matter. But there was a time when you could count on a warm greeting, courteous acknowledgment or at least a hello when you entered a store or place of business you patronized.

Yet, today, in many cases, you're thankful if you can find someone — anyone — in the store to assist you.

I've gone through many a cashier's line where I had to initiate the greeting in hope of finding out if the cashier could indeed speak.

My point is: we've become an age so fast-paced and techno-logical that it's become too impersonal. We just don't pay much attention to one another anymore.

This problem doesn't just occur among those we don't know; it also occurs in our own homes. We are so in tune with progress, and what it can do for us, that we've become out of tune with the human beings around us.

Stop and think about your day yesterday. How much time did you spend having a genuine conversation with another human being? How many people did you pass or encounter whom you didn't even bother to look at? How many times did you return a glance with a smile or a courteous nod of the head as acknowledgement?

Of course I am not suggesting that you walk around grinning all the time while endeavoring to acknowledge everyone you meet. If you did that you would never get where you're going, not to mention what it would do to your facial muscles. What I'm talking about is an attitude or aura you can develop that says; "You don't have to hesitate to talk to me" or "I care about you."

Now you may be thinking to yourself, "What does this have to do with dealing with people who get on your nerves?"

Well to anyone who may be thinking the above, especially at this stage, please keep reading, because you really need this book.

One of the most effective ways to keep from being negatively impacted by the actions or words of another human being is to tune into them.

What do I mean by "tune into"? I'm glad you asked.

I mean you have to take the focus off of you. Don't think about how you feel, what you like or don't like, what you're doing, or where you need to be. You need to slow down and think about the person who is currently getting on your nerves.

This theory works whether you are dealing with a stranger, co-workers, in-laws, a spouse or a child.

If you stopped to pay attention to other people, if only to look them in the eye to ask with incredulity: "what are you doing?" you would instantly feel better towards them.

The reason this works—and it really does—is because the moment you take the focus off of yourself, you are no longer thinking about what those people are doing or how they're affecting you. Instead, you are thinking about them.

We as human beings cannot fully entertain more than one thought at a time. Our feelings are generally indicators of how we are thinking. Therefore, our feelings will change with our focus. Put it to the test.

Right now focus on the first thing you see before you. And I do mean **Focus**. Now see if you can focus on that same thing while you focus on something else.

I know, what a simple example. But illuminating all the same, don't you think?

Illuminating and sometimes frustrating, especially when we wish we could do a dozen things at the same time. On the other hand, it is an advantage, particularly when dealing with people who appear to be extremely annoying or obnoxious individuals.

Chances are, if you consider them annoying or obnoxious, then others probably do also.

So what if instead of the typical reaction, the kind they more than likely expect and receive from most people, you respond differently?

Instead of focusing on how they affect you, focus on their value as a human being. Not only will they no longer have the same effect on you, you may also be a breath of fresh air for these individuals.

You become someone who can look past their personality flaws, bad habits or annoying mannerisms. They may even hate some of these flaws themselves.

This does not necessarily mean that you're going to just grin and play nice. It means that you're going to truly look at this individual in order to discern what you should do to benefit both of you.

And when you cannot think or come up with anything constructive or edifying to say or do, then use my mentor's old adage: "When you don't know what to do, don't do anything at all." Just walk away, but only after you've given them a concerned smile. In other words, do not leave them with an ugly attitude.

Even the "just walk away with a smile" approach should give them something to think about.

If not, it will almost certainly be a different response from what they're use to receiving. And trust me, it will leave you feeling so good about yourself.

Here's an example for you: While driving home, a husband begins to share with his wife his take on an incident that occurred during dinner.

The narrow-minded, chauvinistic view shared by the husband is absolutely nauseating to the wife. But, instead of fussing or walking up one side of him and down the other, she calmly turns to him, looks at him for a moment and says in a loving, nurturing tone, "Baby, I love you, but do you have any idea how obnoxious you sound right now?"

Because she did not say it in anger, disdain or by raising her voice, it was received in a way that actually gave him something to think about.

After a few mumbled words, he simply got quiet and the subject was over. The way the situation was approached left the husband with something to examine about himself and the wife feeling good about how she handled the situation.

Sometimes, we need to look at people simply as children grown up. Just because we become adults does not mean that we cease needing to be nurtured or guided now and then. After all, we are still growing, or at least we should be.

By simply slowing down a little, and focusing less on ourselves, we can drastically change the way we're affected by others.

I know that there are times when it seems no matter how kind, caring or sensitive you are, there are those who seem impossible to reach.

But the operative word here is "seems."

So many times we are negatively affected by others because they are not as we expect them to be.

If we are outgoing and extroverted, we have a tendency to expect the same type of temperament from others.

But, the fact is, there are those who are introverted. It's just not a part of their makeup to react or respond in a certain manner.

So though it may seem that your patience or show of Caring Concern was wasted on a particular individual, chances are it wasn't.

## LOVE OR CARING CONCERN

Most of us are aware of how much all versions of the Bible stress the importance of love. But many are not aware of the type of love to which the Bible refers.

In our culture and language, we use the word "love" to cover all the different types—be it for your child, spouse, friend or parent.

But in other languages, such as those that the Bible was originally written in, there are several words to describe different types of love.

Now, I am not going to give you a mini lesson on Greek or Hebrew. However, I believe the simplest way to understand the type of love the Bible most frequently refers to is by simply replacing the word love with the words "Caring Concern."

Caring Concern is something you can give any living being or creature that exists. You don't have to like the person in order to give it. You don't have to know the person in order to give it. All you have to do is think to yourself, "What if that were me?"

Of course, there are times when we don't love or like ourselves or we get on our own nerves. But we're stuck with ourselves, so what are we gonna do?

Some only dislike themselves some of the time, while caring about themselves most of the time. They will usually give themselves a good talking to, or a tongue lashing, pointing out how unacceptable their action, reaction or comment was. Then they eventually forgive themselves, deal with the consequences and move on.

However, there are those who are just too hard on themselves. These think that they are supposed to be flawless.

Of course, that's not gonna happen as long as they're human. Therefore, they are never satisfied with the person they are or the life they live.

But I have the most empathy for those who have extremely low esteem, which is usually due to their upbringing.

These are the people who never quite get over the things they dislike about themselves. Even worse, they lack the motivation to do anything about it.

Instead, they endeavor to escape through suppression, repression or projection, especially projection. These individuals really have a hard time dealing with the shortcomings of others.

Think about it. If individuals do not care about, tolerate or forgive themselves, how do you imagine they will be with other people? Surely, it's a lot easier to get upset with someone outside of you than with yourself.

In fact, it's the perfect escape for most people. Don't focus on what you need to do to improve yourself, no, that's too hard. That requires too much effort. Just project what you don't like about yourself onto others. Magnify their faults. That way you can feel better about yourself. After all, you've gotta live with you. And, since you're not willing to do the work that would enable you to feel genuinely good about yourself, you've gotta do something to make living with you tolerable, right?

No, it's not right.  But, it is precisely how so many people think, and they're not even aware of it.

Sometimes the right solution is the simplest and most obvious one, but the hardest to accept.

We'll focus more on that point later.

For now, suffice it to say, Caring Concern, for ourselves and for others, is the answer to so many of our problems in this life. You would be amazed at the pain and troubles it can dissolve away.

Want further proof that the above principles and process works?

Ok, think about individuals from your past, men or women that you, for whatever the reason, were smitten with, but for all intents and purposes they were no good for you.  They had all types of problems, issues or hang-ups.

You know what I'm talking about.  I dare say that most, if not all, of us have had an experience with at least one individual who would fall in this category.

Don't you remember how it was obvious to everyone, but you, that you were putting up with far too much from this individual?

Though you eventually came to your senses, you did in fact put up with it, probably longer than you would like to admit. But the question is why.

It's because, for whatever the reason, you saw something in that person that was of value to you.  This person meant something to you, which made it easier to put up with all the drama or hassles this individual produced in your life.

My point is when we care for someone, we naturally put forth the effort to deal with what we don't like about them.

There's always something we don't like about an individual. The issue is how much of that person do we dislike.

Even if your dislike for someone is as high as 90% or more, you can still have Caring Concern for them.  More importantly, they would still be able to sense that you care.

Furthermore, what you don't like about them ceases to have as negative an affect on you because your tolerance level is higher.

Believe it or not, this principle can work with people we don't know and those to whom we're not close. This is due to the power that comes from developing Caring Concern for other human beings in general. And, what's great is that it does not matter who you are, how much money you have or whether you can see, talk, walk, etc. Anyone can develop Caring Concern no matter where or who they are. And in doing so they posses the most powerful ability a human being can apply.

A wonderful thing occurs as you develop the ability to see a human being—any human being—as you would see a sister or a brother. You find that you can deal with their annoying, obnoxious or irritating tendencies with less or no negative affect on yourself.

You know what we put up with from relatives, especially siblings—we put up with stuff that we would not tolerate from any other beings on the planet!

Well, I, for one, believe in the history and accounts preserved in the Bible, as being inspired by and preserved by THE ALMIGHTY.

Therefore, I, of course, believe that the first two humans were created by HIM. With that belief also comes my understanding that all humans, ultimately, are descendants from those original two humans, or at least the ones left after the flood.

**Lucanus's second Treatise (ACTS)** *17:26—HE determined that all humans on the whole earth would be kin through blood.*

Therefore, all humans are a part of me. As distant as the relationship may be, all humans are biologically related. Even scientists have determined, from research, that the DNA of any two human beings is 99.9 percent identical. Therefore, I have a responsibility to care and to do what's right for all individuals.

But, what is the "right" thing to do? In what way am I supposed to treat someone who is nasty or vile? How am I supposed to be towards someone who obviously does not care about me?

Concern or confusion regarding these and similar questions can be a hindrance for many. So we will address these and other questions in a later chapter. For now, I must stress again that I am not talking about playing nice. What we are dealing with here has nothing to do with being polite or politics, from which the word "polite" came.

In fact, one of the problems we face in this age, and especially in this country, is the lack of honesty. We are so concerned about being politically correct that we just throw truth and honesty to the wind.

We cannot grow on lies. You cannot show true Caring Concern for other human beings by lying to them. People have literally killed with niceness. No, not kindness, niceness.

Yes, it's a word; look it up.

What I mean is we hold in too much. We say everything or anything other than what we really think.

I can recall, from several years ago, two co-workers standing around talking about a "friend" of theirs. They were commenting on how she wore down the heels of her shoes to the point where they would damage the wood floors of those whose homes she visited.

Since we were the only ones in the office and I was privy to the conversation, I asked, "Have you ever told her?" They answered "No." I then asked, "Why not?" They answered, "She might get an attitude or upset."

So I shared with them, "If you are truly friends of hers and you care about her, then you would tell her instead of standing here, talking about her behind her back. If she is truly your friend, she may get upset, but ultimately she would get over it and whether she admitted it or not, she would appreciate the honesty."

When I shared this with my co-workers, I was not concerned if what I told them offended them. Because what I told them was the truth and beneficial knowledge that could help them and their friend.

What's also important to interject here is that their concern for how their "friend" would react had nothing to do with consideration for the friend. It was due to their concern about themselves. They did not wish to say anything to her for fear of what she might think of them. "She might get upset with **ME**" or "she might get an attitude with **ME**."

How many times do we find ourselves thinking the same way?

When someone else needs knowledge or understanding, i.e. Truth that could help them, it's not supposed to be about us. It's supposed to be about them and what they need.

When it comes to the subject of honesty with others, someone asked me, "How do you offer honest advice without being misunderstood or without giving off the impression of being self-righteous or condescending?"

First of all, I am not suggesting that we go around pointing out every flaw or fault we see in others. Most people know their faults, at least to an extent. However, when those faults or flaws become so consistent or disruptive that they affect other people, and that includes you, then you need to care enough to bring it to their attention, **regardless of what they might think of you**.

Of course we wish to avoid offending others as much as is humanly possible, but the fact is the truth often offends people, so what do we do—lie to them? When the Bible talks about "giving no offence," it's talking about deliberately doing or saying something unrighteous to another human being that you know will offend them. That's not the type of offence we're talking about here.

The Christ offended people. In what most know as "Matthews" 15:12, The Christ had just finished calling the religious leaders of His time "hypocrites," when one of His disciples came to Him and said, "Do you know that the Pharisees were offended when they heard this?" What, are we greater than The

Christ? What He said to those religious leaders was for their own good and the good of those they affected, **if** they would receive it. But of course they did not; instead they set Him up and had Him turned over to the authorities for execution. Yet, we avoid pointing something out that might be for the good of another, for fear of what they might think of us.

We're talking about showing Caring Concern for others; you simply cannot do that if you're focused more on your own concerns than the person for whom you're supposed to be caring. What makes Caring Concern so powerful and potentially transforming — for both you and the other person — is the self-denial that precedes it.

Nevertheless, in an attempt to avoid causing offence there are a couple of approaches one can use. One approach is to not offer advice; instead, present a question. In most cases you only need one good, thought-provoking question.

I recall a certain co-worker of mine, from years ago, who became notorious around the office for backbiting. This habit of hers became more exasperating by the week, until one day during an office birthday gathering, she came to me and two other co-workers laughing and putting down the fiancée of one of the executives. The fiancée was there for a visit. My co-worker did not know this woman from Eve, yet she saw fit to make fun of her. So I looked at her and asked, "Why do you do that, do you think that you're better than she is?" She really did not know how to answer the question since it was not what she expected. I seem to recall the backbiting coming to a halt after that incident. I know for certain that she never shared any of it with me again, which worked for me.

However, if I had been focused or concerned about what she or the other co-workers might think of me or my question, I would have kept silent, while our notorious office backbiter persisted in getting on everyone's nerves.

The "ask a question" approach works well when you're dealing with someone whose flaws affect you and/or others, which is the primary focus of this book. Though the people affected may not say anything directly to the person at fault, they will often experience relief or satisfaction that somebody else finally said something, so more than likely they will offer you backup or some form of consensus.

But again, you have to care enough to even take the time to come up with a question that might help the person think about their actions or words. But, more importantly, you have to do it without concern for what they may think of you.

We can better deal with others and their shortcomings if we avoid thinking "I-me-isticly." Yes, you won't find it in a dictionary, but this word does not require one. It defines itself.

I-me-istic thinking is disruptive and crippling to all types of relationships, whether the relationship is between mother and child, husband and wife or co-worker to co-worker.

I chose to use I-me-istic instead of the word "self-ish" in order to make sure it's understood that the manner of thinking I am referring to is all about the "I-me." It has nothing to do with the other person.

By the way, I have another made up word to describe what most would refer to as un-self-ish thinking. How about: "You-me-istic."

Webster — look out!

You-me-istic is the way one thinks when one is not just thinking about oneself but also about the other person.

The words I-me-istic and You-me-istic came from the light and inspiration I received through my mentor, to whom this book is dedicated. Due to the humble manner in which she lived her life, I believe she would prefer that I not interject her name here. However, I will say that she was the human instrument my FATHER in Heaven used to raise and nourish me spiritually from the tender age of 19 — and I miss her. ♥

When you are honest with someone out of Caring Concern for that individual and they become offended by it, that's not your problem. If they are offended by the truth delivered to them by someone who has their best interest at heart, then they're the one with the problem.

However, it has been my experience that people are not as easily offended when approached with the truth from one whom they know cares about them.

When you share something with someone out of Caring Concern, it's generally received that way. People can sense your motive. Your delivery is nurturing not hostile or self-righteous.

Even if you are upset with them, it simply comes across differently when you care.

Your Caring Concern is only misconceived when the person simply does not want to know the truth. Under those circumstances you just have to leave it alone.

If you are led to tell them, then do so, but if they turn on you because you endeavored to tell them the truth, then you're off the hook. But at least you put yourself aside by telling them what they needed to know.

You see, once you've informed them, they can never say "I didn't know." They no longer have an excuse. The rest is up to them.

Again, I am not talking about playing nice. I am talking about taking the time to really look and think about the human being (your kinsperson) standing in front of you being obnoxious, malicious or even hateful at the moment.

Instead of letting it get on your nerves, what if you just looked at them for a moment and then said, "You know what (pause) I care about you," and then just walked away. That would not be the reaction they were going for. Not only would you have spared yourself the upset and aggravation you would have experienced had you given into their ploy, you would have manifested something they probably needed desperately to see: Caring Concern.

*Though I speak with the language of humans and of cherubim, and do not have caring concern, I shall be as sounding brass, or a tinkling cymbal. Though I have the gift of foresight, and understand all mysteries, and all knowledge; though I have belief that could move mountains, and have not caring concern, I am nothing. Though I bestow all my goods to feed the poor, and though I give my body to be burned, and have not caring concern, it will profit me nothing*

**Caring concern means I suffer long, and am kind; I will not envy; I will not be arrogant, or puffed up. I will not behave unseemly, nor seek only my own way; I will not be easily provoked, nor will I think evil. I will not rejoice in inequity, but will rejoice in the truth. I will bear many things, believe many things; hope in many things, and endure many things. Caring concern will not be unsuccessful;** *but whether there be foresight, it shall be in part; whether there be languages, they shall cease; whether there be knowledge, it shall vanish away.*

*For we know in part, and we foresee in part. But when that which is complete has come, then that which is in part shall not be needed. When I was a child, I spoke as a child, I understood as a child, I thought as a child; but when I grew up, I put away childish things. Right now it's like we see through a glass obscurely; but soon we shall see HIM face to face; now I know in part, but then I shall know even as also I am known.*

*What I now have is belief, hope, and caring concern, these three; but the greatest of these is caring concern.*

# NOTES

# Chapter 3

## When People Get On Your Nerves At Work

## CO-WORKERS

I RECALL YEARS AGO, when working as an administrative assistant, that one of my co-workers (we'll call her "Looney"), for whatever the reason, had it in for me. Some thought she was envious, though I can't imagine why.

She would smile in my face, but at every opportunity she would say or do something to express just how much she disliked me.

While I was on vacation, Looney was assigned to cover my work area. As she sat at my workstation, another co-worker walked by only to observe Looney changing all of the defaults set on my computer's monitor. The observing co-worker asked if she was doing it because she thought it was necessary and thus intended to change it back or if it was out of spite. Looney admitted that it was indeed done out of spite.

When I returned to work from vacation, to my consternation I found my computer monitor's default colors changed to the point where it looked as if someone had thrown up in there.

It was frightful.

Keep in mind, I was young and at an immature stage of my spiritual growth. Yet, I had been taught at an early age about the perils of giving in to one's impulses, such as anger or revenge, which helped me a great deal that day. So did my wish to keep my job.

Otherwise, I may have given in to anger, not just for this incident but everything else I had to put up with from Ms. Looney, and simply beaten the daylights out of her. But, of course, I did not, nor was I inclined to do so.

However, she didn't know that.

So I was cool. I found her alone in the office lunchroom. I walked in, closing the door behind me as I stood up against it. There we stood, just her and me. I knew I had evoked fear in her because she began ranting and raving about her mood and that she was not to be messed with.

Once she was done, I calmly said: "It's very disconcerting to return from vacation and find your monitor tampered with." I paused for a moment and then continued to say, "Don't let it happen again." I then calmly turned around and left.

I could just feel the sigh of relief she experienced as I left the room. She had no idea what I would do.

To my delight, Ms. Looney left the company just a few months later. However, she was not the only co-worker in that office with big time issues.

In fact, I have never, before or since, worked in an environment where there were so many miserable people. If it had been my first job or if I had never worked in any other office environment, I probably would have left there with a terrible complex or the belief that I lacked some sort of ability to get along with others.

The stories I could tell you of my experiences there would simply amaze you.

But, since that would require a book twice the size of this one, let's just not go there.

What made it all bearable was the relationship I had with my manager, whom I loved, and her assistant manager, whom I liked a lot.

However, what really enabled me with the resolve to persevere was the power of THE ALMIGHTY, the work experience I would acquire, and my attitude.

You see, I was not there to teach my co-workers the error of their ways or the 1001 reasons why they should like me. I was there to do my job to the best of my ability in order to get paid.

I don't mean that I was not cordial or that I ignored people. On the contrary, I endeavored to treat each of my co-workers in the same manner I would wish to be treated—most of the time. Again, I was young.

However, my focus was on my job and not my social status.

Therefore, I did not spend the company's time socializing. I was not getting paid to become popular. It wasn't high school. I was paid to do the job for which I was hired.

By thinking in that manner, I was able to care about the people I worked with, without permitting their attitudes to affect me—again, most of the time.

Though we all wish to be liked, it wasn't part of my job requirement. The only thing that mattered was my ability to work with my co-workers? Since I did care about them and they were aware of that, we were able to manage. And, though I was not popular with many, I am pretty certain that I had gained their respect.

I worked with these people for four years. It was difficult; it was frustrating, and there were times when it was painful because I did care for each and every one of them. But it was also one of the most growth-inducing experiences of my life, and I would not trade it for anything. I learned, I grew, and when the time was right, I moved on.

The point is I don't know what your particular work experience is, but I do know that however you deal with co-workers, no matter what their issues or hang ups may be, the quality of your work experience is up to you.

Your attitude and how you handle yourself is all that matters. A job is just that, a job. If you go with the attitude of being the best you can be at what you do, I can guarantee you won't have much time for the drama.

Whether your co-workers like you or not, they will respect you and treat you like a professional due to your professional attitude.

More importantly, your employer will also, which should result in higher pay raises or promotions.

Imagine what your opponents would think if you became their manager. Hmmm.

Nevertheless, most of us spend the majority of our lifetimes at our jobs. Therefore, if you are truly unhappy where you are or if management is really a problem, then don't falsely justify why you should stay; do what you have to do.

Find time to look for another position, and once you have, leave.

However, make sure that you have examined yourself thoroughly. Be absolutely honest when you ask yourself: "Is there anything I could do differently to make my situation better, without leaving my current job?"

You may also wish to ask others whom you trust for an honest assessment of your job performance, attitude and habits. Make sure that it's not you instead of your job that needs changing.

Find out if you are either a Duck or an Eagle.

## DUCKS & EAGLES

In the world of fowls, Ducks and Eagles are opposites in nature. In essence, Eagles sore, while Ducks, though they can fly, have a tendency to stay very close to earth.

You find Ducks floating about on a lake or wherever they may find calm waters. When watching them, it appears as if they're just sitting there. However, if the water is clear enough, many times you can see their little webbed feet paddling away. They are extremely passive fowl. Not very assertive or aggressive.

Whatever they eat has to be close to the earth also, or under water, such as insects, fish and plants.

The Eagle, however, is a predator. It's the lion of the fowl world. You won't find an Eagle settling for insects and plants. They go after much bigger game. In fact, the Bald Eagle eats Ducks. When they get their claws into something, they don't let go until they can place their prey on a solid, secure surface.

I think both Ducks and Eagles are beautiful creatures, and I appreciate them both.

So why am I telling you about Ducks and Eagles?  Because, metaphorically speaking, humans are either Ducks or Eagles.

Have you ever approached store employees for help with finding something only to receive a somewhat glazed look, accompanied by shoved shoulders, as they sit, turning their heads slowly from side to side, indicating they have no clue or the desire to put forth the effort to find out?

If you have, the employees whose help you sought were Ducks.  Hence, in this instance, you have your "Sitting Ducks." You see, an Eagle could not respond in that manner, even on a bad day.

Eagles are self-driven individuals.  Using our above example, an Eagle, after admitting that he or she wasn't sure of the answer to your question, would have either picked up the store's phone to contact someone who could help you or escorted you to the appropriate person.

Ducks do just enough to get by.  People who are Ducks have no problem getting paid for doing nothing, if they can get away with it.

Ducks look at a challenge and say it can't be done.  Eagles look at a challenge and say there's got to be a way.

When you call the customer service department of a business you patronize and the service representative is telling you how something cannot be done, don't get frustrated or raise your voice to the representative.  You may be dealing with a Duck. Simply ask the representative for their name and then ask for a supervisor.  More than likely the supervisor will be an Eagle.

I say that because most people in leadership positions got there by being Eagles.  In my experience, it is extremely rare to get a supervisor who quacks.

You also won't find an Eagle in a dead end job.  Because Eagles don't settle, they move up.  Employers promote Eagles.

Why?

Because they take esteem in whatever they do and therefore do a great job.

Smart employers will do whatever they can to keep an Eagle

happy, because they know that Eagles are hard to find.

I recall looking for boots in a mall once. I came across a shoe shop, where there was only one store clerk minding the store and I was her only customer. I thought this was great! I could get in and out.

Now, one would think it terrible for a store clerk to talk on the telephone the entire time she attended to a customer, right?

Then what would one's opinion be of a store clerk who talked on two telephones while waiting on a customer.

Yes, she did!

In one hand she held what appeared to be the store's phone and, simultaneously, she somehow managed to talk with someone else on her cell phone. She did all that while attempting to attend to me.

I've heard of the "multitasking generation," but this was multi-ridiculous!

There was no manager or supervisor there, and I was already frustrated. I had walked all over the mall looking for boots that didn't have chop sticks for heels. So I merely left the store as she continued to chat away.

However, on my way out of the mall, as I headed back toward the store, I glanced inside. She was still on the phone. So I waited, not to buy boots but to talk to her. She was young, and I thought she could use a little wake up call.

She never actually hung up the phone, but she did eventually respond to my presence in the store. I smiled and asked if she was in school. She said, "Yes." "What's your major?" I asked. She answered, "Business." "Really?" I said. "Do you plan to own your own business one day?" "Yes," she answered. I calmly and quietly said to her, "Tell me something, what if you decided, after college, to open a store, how would you feel if the one employee that you trusted to run your store lost customers in your absence, because she talked continually on the phone instead of doing the job she was paid to do?"

I didn't wait for an answer. As she realized my point, her initial smile disappeared, and, after telling her to take care, so did I.

Now, one might think that I was being mean to this stranger.

But this is what I was referring to in the previous chapter. This young lady was not a stranger. Though we had never met before, she was my daughter, or niece or babysitter. In other words, she was someone I cared about.

There was no one else there to witness what was going on or to give her the opportunity to think about what she was doing.

She was, in fact, stealing from the owner, among other things. The owner was not paying her to talk on the phone, especially with customers in the store. Had it been her own business, she certainly would not tolerate anyone doing what she was doing to another business owner.

I could have held my tongue, out of concern for what she might think of me, and complained about her to myself or to others behind her back — but how would that help her?

She was young and in school. She had a future before her — in business no less!

Hopefully, because I cared enough to make an honest point, she will, at least, feel some degree of conviction the next time she's on the phone and a customer walks in.

I don't know if she took advantage of that opportunity to see and change. I don't know if she went on to develop into an Eagle, thus losing the Duck attitude that contributed to her poor job performance.

What I do know is, because of what was pointed out to her that day, she can never honestly say she wasn't aware or didn't know.

We as human beings cannot do differently until we know differently. But once we know, then we are without excuse.

Think about the above question, "Are you a Duck or an Eagle?" If you are honest enough with yourself to answer that question accurately, you can move on to becoming whatever you want to be.  Unlike real Ducks, human Ducks can become Eagles.

If you have examined yourself regarding your job and came to the conclusion that the problem is not the job or the other workers but it's you, then **Congratulations!**  You have reason to celebrate.

Huh?  What?

Yes, Celebrate!   You've just discovered that your future success in your present job is totally within your control.

Therefore, you don't have to go through what it takes to find a new job.  You don't have to be concerned about what anyone else is doing.  That's *Wonderful!*

If the problem were outside of yourself, you wouldn't have control over it.  There would be little if anything you could do.  For example, if it were a manager who disliked you for some reason and treated you unfairly, what could you do?

You certainly don't have control over the manager, unless you came across some dark secret of his, forcing him to give you control or else!

However, since this is not fiction or a screenplay, let's just stick with what's usually the case.

The fact is we don't have control over what other people do or think.   Only if other human beings give us control, for whatever their reasons, do we have any power over them.

So if the person is not small enough to pick up and carry away, forget about it.  Even then it's hard to do if it's an un-willing participant.

If you are your own problem, you can control you.   It requires a great deal of effort on your part.  But the point is it can be done **if** you want it bad enough.

If you determine that you're a Duck, then you simply need to do whatever it will take to develop into an Eagle.

The focus of this book is not that particular process.

However, I am working on another book entitled "**Cold Turkey**."  Its mission will be to show its readers how to use the power of THE ALMIGHTY, along with their own longing, to transform their lives wherever it's needed.    We're thinking about making the subtitle:

### "From Sloth to Disciplined in 90 days"

But enough of the commercial, let's get back to the purpose of the book you're now reading.

If you gain and develop the ability to take an honest, accurate look at yourself, you will find that your co-workers, who used to really get on your nerves, don't have the same effect on you. In fact, you may find that they don't affect you at all.

However, the key is to take an HONEST look.  For most, that means input from output.

Have you ever considered the fact that we as human beings would not have a clue as to what our faces looked like if it were not for the aid of something outside of ourselves?

No human has ever looked directly on his or her own face, except via a reflection from something outside of themselves.

So imagine how hard it must be to honestly see ourselves from within, without outside help.

Anyone with a discerning eye can see you better than you can see yourself.   The question is will they care enough to honestly tell you what they see?

Hopefully, there are those in your life who would.  Of course, once they do, the rest is up to you.

If it comes to light that you are indeed a Duck, and you don't accept it and endeavor to change, then neither will your circumstances.  You will simply go from job to job, only to experience the same things over and over again.  Because, no matter where you go, you will always be with you.

However, if you accept the truth and develop into an Eagle, chances are, you won't have problems with co-workers, at least nothing you can't handle, because your focus will be on your job.

When a person is determined to earn their pay, they will always find something to do. If they can't find anything, they go to their employer or supervisor asking for work.

They are not comfortable getting paid for doing nothing.

Think of the respect that type of attitude would warrant from their employer.

The bottom line is when it comes to co-workers who may get on your nerves, learn to focus on what you're paid to do.

I am certain you will find that you simply won't have the time for anything else.

## WORKING WITH THE PUBLIC:

When it comes to people getting on your nerves, one might think that working with the public would be the most challenging.

Well, it depends on how you look at it. On one hand, you are exposed to a variety of personalities, temperaments and mood swings.

On the other hand, your encounters, unlike those with your co-workers, are limited. Even if you have customers who visit your facility daily, more than likely they won't stay very long, which means you only have to endure whatever challenges these individuals may present for a short period of time. In most cases, you will never see the customer again.

Nevertheless, it takes a certain type of individual to work successfully with the public.

I believe we often run into disgruntled or disinterested employees because many public positions require few qualifycations. Therefore, lots of individuals working with the public are doing so not due to a preference for the work but because that's all they're able to get at the time.

If that isn't an argument for getting a good education or going to college, I don't know what is.

To have to cater to numerous people, day after day, because you can't qualify for a job that would really suit you is a miserable way to live. This sad fact is especially true when you consider how much time we spend, throughout our lives, working.

If this describes you, I have four words for you: GO BACK TO SCHOOL. Figure out what would make you happy and GO BACK TO SCHOOL. One very good thing about this country is that funding or loans are available for anyone who wants to learn.

Though you must pay it back, a student loan is the easiest of loans for which you can qualify. Uncle Sam wants you to get the education you need. If you have the discipline, you don't need a classroom for many degrees or training. You can learn and earn your degree online.

So if it's at all possible, go for it. You may be surprised at how interesting learning will be, regardless of how boring it seemed when you were in school. Don't underestimate yourself.

On the other hand, if it's not possible, you may wish to check out a book titled *What Color is Your Parachute?* by Richard Nelson Bolles. Bolles shares some very innovative and unorthodox ways to successfully find the type of job you want and effective ways to make career changes.

Jobs or positions that don't require work with the public are limited, but they are out there. Make a list of them. Hopefully you can pick one that will make getting out of bed in the morning worth your while.

But until you can complete your training and find the position you want, you have to deal with what you have. Perhaps the following will help you to cope better.

When I think of working with the public, I think of a particular post office worker I know. In spite of the terrible stigma cast upon postal workers in the past, this one worker is a ray of sunshine. In fact, that's what I call her: "Sunshine."

We all know how relatively quick postal transactions can take place. Once you actually get to the window, you're usually in and out. Yet, within that small frame of time, Sunshine manages to treat you like family.

I find that even when I am feeling out of it, her pleasant attitude picks me up. She is absolutely refreshing.

Believe it or not, most people feel this way when they encounter public workers who appear to not only care about how well they do their jobs, but also about you, the customer.

At this point you should be seeing a pattern. Caring Concern for other human beings, whether we know them personally or not, cannot be unsuccessful. It works in all situations.

In my early twenties, I worked for a small health food chain. I recall a young guy who came in every day for our trail mixes.

This guy always looked as if he might bite into your face if you dared to utter an unnecessary word. So I'm sure that most found him intimidating or unapproachable.

But I was never one to be easily intimidated, so I would engage him in conversation. I asked him once, "Why do you look so mean when you come in here?"

He didn't even realize how miserable he looked. I don't recall how the initial conversation went, but I do recall how beautiful his smile was once I finally got it out of him. When he smiled I saw that he was a pretty nice-looking guy.

In fact, totally to my surprise, he ultimately asked me to lunch, which led to a bowling date and, eventually, a good friend. I don't remember exactly how we lost touch.

My point is 90% of the time when you show people that you care, they will expose the better side of themselves.

You, as one who works with the public, are in a position to make a difference in the life of each individual you encounter. A person is affected when they encounter another human being who thinks that they are important enough to care about.

I have gone through cashier lines in which my entire encounter would have been with the cashier's eyelids had I not initiated some sort of greeting.

Sometimes, as I'm leaving the line, I find myself tempted to say, "Thank you, please come again."

Hey, I figure since the cashier's not speaking, somebody ought to say it.

It really does make a difference in people's lives when another human being smiles at them, puts forth the effort to call them by their name or comments on how nice they look.

Merchants and businesses know this. They endeavor to train their public representatives on how to be courteous and helpful to customers. They know that in doing so the customers will want to continue to do business with them. In other words, they want you to make the customer feel special because it's good for business.

But, putting capitalism aside, take the time to think about how it makes you feel when you're treated well or made to feel special by a complete stranger.

Then make it your goal and responsibility to help others feel that way. Not only will you be praised and valued highly by your employer, you will also make a great contribution to humankind.

As corny as that might sound, it's true.

People have to deal with enough ugliness in this world; why not be instrumental in contributing to what's beautiful about life. It certainly will make your job more rewarding.

Your job will cease to be just about a paycheck. It will become about the very people you serve each day. When it does, you'll notice just how seldom people get on your nerves.

## FOR BUSINESS OWNERS

I have spent most of my adult life as an entrepreneur, so I do have a word or two to share with business owners and/or managers.

I am speaking of individuals who employ or may supervise both Ducks and Eagles.

First of all, I know how frustrating it is to be in a position where you have to depend on others to successfully conduct your business.

However, if you are in this position, I assume you have the temperament for it. The question is: how is it affecting your nervous system?

Business owners are Eagles by default. You simply don't venture into owning your own business if you are a Duck. Ducks would not dream of taking on the responsibility or exerting the discipline it takes to make it as a business owner.

That's certainly not to say that everyone who works for an employer is a Duck. Nothing could be farther from the truth.

My point is that those who do successfully build or run their own businesses are Eagles. It is an absolute prerequisite.

Therefore, as an Eagle, you, the business owner, may do a fabulous job of holding in and holding back, so as not to offend or experience too much turnover.

However, it is my opinion that as a business owner with employees, you have a greater responsibility to your employees than to simply grin and bear it.

In fact, once you make it absolutely clear what you want and will not tolerate, you should get what you require.

Why? Because it's your business. Of course, I'm assuming that you're not breaking any laws, and you treat people fairly.

Because of your business, you have an opportunity not only to provide jobs but also to guide, influence and teach those whom you employ.

Owning a business, in and of itself, is a pretty huge responsibility. Owning a business that employs others is an enormous responsibility, multiplied by each person you employ.

It requires a lot more than just a head for business.

I recall an incident I experienced during my "Stupid Stage" — that's what I call the period most teens experience between the ages of 13 and 16. Though it might start sooner and end later these days.

I was 16. A nearby restaurant was looking for another waitress, and I got the job. It was my second place of employment.

My manager and I got along great, though I believe our rapport may have been largely due to the crush he had on my mom. He met her one evening when she decided to dine at the restaurant with me as her server.

However, not long after getting the job, I was introduced to a new supervisor; we'll refer to him as the General. He had authority over my regular manager. In fact, though he wasn't actually a General, he had been my manager's commanding officer while in the military.

My regular manager talked about how tough the General was back then. Yet he seemed like a real sweet guy to me. I had no doubt that I would be able to wrap him around my little finger, just as I had done with my regular manager.

The General called me into his office one day. He informed me that he was having a hard time making out the numbers on my receipts. He was particular concerned with the way I wrote the number five (5). He said it looked like the letter "S."

So I'm thinking, "Yeah right, that's important, and by the way, GET A LIFE!"

Sometime later he called me in again regarding the same thing. Each time he was calm and gentle in his approach. And, each time, I would smile and joked around about the whole issue.

We actually got along well. I found him easy to be around and honestly thought he liked me in an Uncle and Niece kinda way.

Still later, he brought me in a third time. Again, keep in mind, I was a sixteen-year-old teenager.

So, by now I'm thinking, "SERIOUSLY, how important is this? There are no other numbers that resemble the letter **S**. So if you see what appears to be an **S** in the middle of a set of numbers, then it must be (come on, say it with me) that's right: the number **5**. Duhhh!"

Of course, I didn't actually say any of this out loud. But when you think a certain way, generally your body language and attitude will give a hint of what's on your mind.

Nevertheless, the next time he called me into his office he gave me my walking papers. When I asked him why, he shared with me how he had told me, three times, to better define the number five (5) on my receipts. That was the only reason he gave for firing me.

Thirty-four (34) years later, I am able to share this incident with such detail because of what I gained from the experience.

I would like to believe that my supervisor saw potential in me and, due to my young age, took that opportunity to teach me a very valuable lesson. The fact is I don't know if those were his intentions or not.

However, I do know that he succeeded in doing just that.

I would go on to never forget the experience. And boy, did I learn from it.

Subsequently, though I give thanks always first to my FATHER in Heaven for how well HE continues to raise me through various experiences, I would also like to take this opportunity to express my thanks to the General.

When it comes to employees and employers, one could easily take the "it's business" attitude or stance.

However, I believe if you want your life to really mean something you have to take it a bit further than that.

I know I am beginning to sound like a broken record, but the bottom line again is: you have to care.

I don't think anyone could appreciate more than I how hard it is to find Eagles or even reliable Ducks. I also understand that one is in business to make money.

But when there are human beings involved and you oversee them and thus, in many ways, are responsible for them, you have to think about the bigger picture.

For your sake and theirs you have to make it absolutely clear what you require and what you find unacceptable. Most importantly, you must be consistent.

You have to say what you mean and mean what you say if you wish to minimize the stress of having to supervise employees. By doing so, you also teach responsibility and consistency to your staff.

Pay close attention to what you're about to read in Chapter IV regarding sentiment. As you do, keep in mind that one cannot manage or run a business with sentiment. One can, however, run a business with compassion and equity. In fact, it's the only way one should run a business.

As for the health of your nervous system, here's something to think about: if you have policies and guidelines in place that make it clear what is and is not acceptable, how can your employee(s) go as far as to get on your nerves?

Unless, of course, you are not following your own rules or you run your business like a day care instead of an establishment where you employ adults.

When starting a business, I truly believe that one should include as part of their business plan the time it will take to find the right people. This time is especially needed when you are a part of an industry in which Eagles are extremely hard to find.

To that challenge, I say: regardless of the industry, you get what you pay for, and Eagles are not cheap.

Nevertheless, even Eagles will not thrive if the business owner or manager is inconsistent regarding what's expected of them.

The role of management is actually far more crucial than many may realize.

In fact, be it a school, store or office, if you wish to know what the overall atmosphere and attitude of an establishment is, simply go straight to management or whoever is in charge.

There you will find the heart of that business. If the heart is not functioning well, you can be assured that its issues will be reflected throughout the entire staff.

It's your business or organization; therefore, you are going to be faced with all types of problems. However, if you run it with Caring Concern, equity and consistency, employees who get on your nerves will not be one of them.

## BUSINESS OWNERS AND THEIR CUSTOMERS

So what if you don't have employees?  Perhaps you own the type of business that enables you to work alone.  You don't need employees.  A secretary or administrative assistant might be nice, but not necessary.  You only have clients or customers to which to tend.

Well, when it comes to the subject of patience or tolerance for others, don't you think it's amazing that no matter how obnoxious or ridiculous your customers may behave, somehow you're able to quickly and effectively find a way to tolerate whatever they say or do?

Why is that?  It's because without customers, your business has no business.

This portion of the chapter was added in order to bring home a very important point made earlier.

The point is business owners, who are dependent upon customers to stay in business, can find patience, control and tolerance they never knew they had.

In fact, any business owner who's been in that position for a long length of time has developed, out of necessity, the ability to deal with the most challenging of personalities.

A rooky real estate agent, while attending her first closing, sat in the title company's conference room along with her clients and sales manger.

During the process of closing the deal, an issue arose regarding the property.  Before they knew it, the sellers and the buyers became quite agitated, exchanging a few heated words. The rooky agent sat there terrified that the deal was not going to close.  She began to express her anxiety when her sales manager, a seasoned agent who had been in the business for years, signaled her to just keep quiet, remain calm and wait.

She followed her manager's advice.  Within minutes, the title attorney intervened, brought everything under control and the deal closed successfully.

I'm sure there was a time when the sales manger was not so confident or composed. But time and necessity had taught her that patience and tolerance (a.k.a. longsuffering) pays.

Again, this goes back to what we covered earlier. Whether it's to hold on to a mate or a customer, one's ability to show tolerance or Caring Concern is enhanced when we can see how it behooves us. Believing it's in our best interest to develop Caring Concern towards every human being we meet could actually safeguard our nervous systems and several other organs from much undue stress or irritation.

This next example is a little off the focus for this chapter, but I can't think of a better time to use it.

A young mother of three would often come to me regarding her inability to demonstrate patience with her children. She could not understand how she managed to be so patient with others but not with her own children.

The problem for this mother was the same as it is for so many parents. She cared about the impression she made on others or what they might think if she spoke or behaved unseemly.

However, when it came to her children, it simply didn't matter as much. If she were to make a vicious comment to one of her children, they would not retaliate as an adult or the parent of another child might.

Therefore, she was not as motivated to display patience or tolerance toward these little people who relied on her example. This is the same attitude we have when it comes to people we do not know or think we may never see or talk to again.

However, if we practiced having Caring Concern for **everyone** we met, we would gradually find it easier to tolerate some of the crazy, rude, and sometimes ridiculous things people do, preserving our nervous systems in the process.

*Why behold the splinter that is in your neighbor's eye, and do not even think about the beam that is in your own eye? Or, why say to your neighbor: Let me remove the splinter from your eye; and, do nothing to remove the beam from your own eye? Do not be hypocrites; first remove the beam that is in your own eye; and then you can see clearly to remove the splinter that is in your neighbor's eye.\*\*\*\*\**

# NOTES

# Chapter 4

## When People Get On Your Nerves At Home

THERE IS NO group of people, on the face of the earth, that can pluck my nerves as intensely as my relatives can.

I address this subject because I tend to believe that many reading this book may feel the same way.

It's not because we don't love or cherish our relatives. It's largely due to the ongoing history we have with these people. We've accumulated years of offences, conflicts and emotional injury. Yet, because they're family, we tend to find some way to put up with it all.

The problem is, though we may put our issues aside when it comes to family members, most of us never really resolve them.

Consequently, we treat those issues like balloons held under water. Eventually, we get tired of keeping it all down. So up they float to the surface, popping all over the place, making an absolute mess at the most inappropriate times.

There's another reason why relatives can get on our nerves, more so than others; we often see in them what we don't like about ourselves. This is due to our biological connection in addition to the other influences they've had in our lives.

Recently, I went out with my mother to take her to the airport.

When we arrived, I obtained the information I needed from the clerk working the outside check-in counter.

My mother, however, did not wish to accept the instructions the clerk provided. She insisted that he was wrong and only wanted to receive a tip.

Finally, I convinced her to get out of the van so she could check in. As she approached the clerk, I took note of her disposition and attitude. She was still not convinced that he knew what he was doing.

Her approach and attitude toward him was somewhat condescending, and it made me, literally, sick to my stomach.

There was a time when I would have made matters worse by lashing out at her for such a disdainful display. But I had become aware of why situations like this one disturbed me so deeply.

There, with the check-in-clerk, my mother manifested traits I hated within myself.

I had developed the ability to recognize it, and many other things within me, due to my relationship with my FATHER in Heaven and HIS Son. Though it is a lifelong process, my daily goal and purpose for living is to put on the character of my FATHER in place of my own, which makes understanding who I am and what I am capable of (good or bad) absolutely mandatory. In fact, I believe it is a mandate for anyone professing to follow The Christ.

But where do we start?

I'm sure you've seen on television or read in books how psychiatrists or therapists always ask the patient about their parents, especially their mothers.

They generally start there because, though it's not impossible, it is extremely challenging for people to truly understand themselves without knowing their parents.

So much of our temperament and tendencies come from our parents, whether they were responsible for raising us or not.

I will never forget watching a program aimed at proving this point. One young man, who had never met his father, found his dad at the age of thirty something. After meeting and learning a little about him, he discovered that they were remarkably alike. They had the same taste in clothing (they each liked to dress like cowboys), the same taste in women and countless other similarities.

My experience with my own dad convinced me of how much the general make-up and temperament of our parents affect us, even when we don't know the parent.

Though I knew my dad, I did not *know* him. I was raised by my mom.  It was not until I became fifty that he and I committed to spending quality time together.

In doing so, I discovered the source of so many of my mannerisms and characteristics.  I am actually more like my dad than my mom, which explains a lot.

There's no doubt about it; genetics has a great deal to do with who we are.

This is especially true when it comes to our inclinations and temperaments.  Our temperaments have a tremendous effect on how we relate to others.

For years, I did not understand why my mother could affect me the way she did.  Once I became an adult, we would get into shouting matches that left me laden with guilt.

There was no doubt that I had affection for her and cared about her.  She's actually quite precious to me.

However, only after I understood that she was not my problem was I able to spend extended periods of time with her, while remaining reasonably calm.

I could now witness her attitude toward the check-in clerk and know that I was capable of the same attitude. I was aware of those times when it rose up within me, and I hated that it could.  I knew and had seen how ugly it was, but still it was in me to feel that way.

Once I stopped beating myself up and accepted that I was not a terrible person, I could recognize where the attitude or inclination stemmed from.  Armed with that understanding, I was ready to take it on.

No one had to tell me that the attitude was not right.  I even knew how I needed to think in order to combat or replace any thoughts that would encourage it.

Yet, with everything I knew or understood about what can evoke thoughts and feelings, I did not understand why I could not permanently prevent the tendency toward that type of disposition.

I finally came to see and accept that it was simply a part of my temperament, contributed not only by my mother but also by my dad, who also had those tendencies.

Now, though I still hate when it raises its ugly head, I know that I must accept all the different aspects of me. However, that does not mean that I have to give in to them all.

It's like knowing and accepting that you have a spoiled child. Regardless of how he or she got that way, you do not have to continue to give into the child.

It's so important to understand that the people who were once members of our household, people who were a dominant or consistent presence in our lives, are still a part of us to one degree or another. If we accept that, we can get to know ourselves on levels most never reach.

We would learn to better love and appreciate ourselves and the very family members we found it hard to tolerate.

As for all that we've suffered or endured due to experiences with our relatives, one must either get on it or get over it. For as long as you repress or suppress whatever it is, not only will Aunt Lulu get on your nerves but so will anyone who reminds you of Aunt Lulu.

## SUPPRESION & REPRESSION

When getting to know and understand oneself, there are two words in the English language I believe we should know and understand. Therefore, this portion of this chapter focuses on these words and their meanings:

> **SUPPRESSION:** a mental process occurring when one refuses to deal with or address an issue, feeling or impulse. It involves an aware, intentional suppression (i.e., holding down) of specific thoughts or feelings.

As demonstrated previously, the process is a lot like holding down balloons under water, but instead of balloons, certain thoughts or feelings are suppressed.

It's a common practice that requires a lot of energy. When used for the wrong reasons, it can result in the manifestation of certain symptoms such as fatigue, high blood pressure, ulcers, etc.

**REPRESSION:** is pretty much the same as suppression, with one exception. When one uses repression, they do so without awareness. However, it can bring about the same results and physical symptoms as suppression.

When it comes to honesty, neither suppression nor repression is the answer.

I cannot stress enough how important it is to understand who we are and what causes us to do the things we do, say or think.

Since our thoughts will evoke most of what we feel, it's especially important to be aware of how we think. In essence, we must learn to be honest with ourselves.

We cannot grow on lies, be it from others or ourselves. When we understand, accept and care for whom we are, we find it much easier to care for others.

When The Christ said that one's enemies would be those of their own household *(Matthew 10:36),* I believe that those words spoke of both our physical and spiritual households.

We must explore the fears and impulses that come from members of our household within.

You can be certain that when we are **easily** annoyed or exasperated by other human beings, the problem does not lie from without but from within us. If you are one who is frequently irritated by others, I challenge you to a test.

The next time you encounter someone who affects you in that manner, stop and examine exactly what it was the person did to provoke or annoy you.

Then ask yourself three questions:

1) **Was it something you have a tendency to do?**
   *If so,*
2) **Is it something you do not like about yourself?**
   *or,*
3) **Was it something you believe you would never do?**

If you realize that it's something that you also do and dislike about yourself, you have only to apply the principles we've already covered.

However, if it's something you think or feel you would never do, well, that requires a slightly different look at yourself.

While in my early twenties, I had a friend who was the manager of an ice cream shop. Her employees were young people, most of them still in high school. I recall the day she discovered that two employees had been stealing (eating) the store's ice cream. She was outraged. It was appalling to her that these high school students would eat some of the ice cream without paying for it. She fired them both.

Now, I certainly don't condone stealing, and, after my experience with the General, I thought since they were young and had little to lose, firing them might help them do better in the future.

However, it was her indignation over the matter that got my attention. So I asked if she had ever stolen anything. She replied with an even more indignant "NO, Never!"

Though I was not wise enough to think of it at the time, my next question should have been: "Have you ever lied?" To which she definitely would have answered, "Yes," unless she lied of course.

I then could have asked, "What's the difference?"

My friend could look with disdain at anyone who would steal because she would never do anything so dishonest. Yet she would lie.

THE ALMIGHTY does not distinguish between the two. HE disapproves of both, so what right did she have to her disdain?

If self-evaluation reveals that you are often annoyed by people who do things you would never do, think about the various things you do. If you cannot think of anything that would fall under the category of being annoying or irritating to others, just ask around.

Again, we're back to the same conclusions:

- If you want people to stop getting on your nerves, then learn to care more about them.
- If you want to care more about people, then learn to care more about yourself.
- If you want to care more about yourself, then learn to be honest with yourself and who you are.
- Then give yourself permission to have Caring Concern for every aspect of you.

Developing true Caring Concern for yourself first is the foundation that will affect the way you view others, be it relatives, co-workers or strangers.

Let's take a closer look at how we can live in peace with ourselves.

## THE MEMBERS OF YOUR OWN HOUSEHOLD

Those who have had the greatest influence in your life, whether living or deceased, are still with you. Once you become an adult, how often you see or speak with those individuals doesn't matter. They are already a part of you, and they can still influence your life.

Also, you still have the child and the adolescent you once were within you.  They too continue to influence your life, sometimes in ways you're opposed to.

That's right, the people and experiences that you may think you've left behind are still influencing, perhaps even dominating, your life **IF** you are not in control of your own household.

Years ago, after walking to the store alone, I was about to leave with my small bag of groceries when I saw a group of pre-teen girls standing outside the only exit from the store.  They were pretty angry-looking kids. Though I did not know them, they reminded me of the girls I went to school with, the same girls I had managed to avoid throughout elementary school, the same girls who would pick fights with me for no apparent reason.

I stood there stricken with fear as I hesitated to leave the store.

Now you may be thinking that I am speaking of a late childhood or teenage experience. But, in fact, I was a grown woman in my late twenties when this occurred.

However, it was not I, the woman, who hesitated to leave the store.  It was the young girl in me who was terrorized by her peers in elementary school.  If I had not recognized that quickly, I may have come to the conclusion that I was losing my mind.

Instead, as I stood there, I realized how the eight-year-old child in me was afraid.  She had grown up as an only child, yet she had managed to escape the girls who used to threaten to beat her up and cut her face.

She had moved away with her mother out of the neighborhood before the girls could make good on their threats. Obviously, the gathering outside the store that day evoked a fearful childhood memory.  If during my childhood, I had not been afraid of having my face marred for life and actually fought my dreaded foes while in elementary school, I'm sure the feelings I experienced that day would not have been the same.  But even as a child, I felt it was just too great a price to pay, especially since I had no say as to where I would live or whether I wished to attend one of the roughest elementary schools in the area. So, unless I was cornered with no way out, I ran!

Once I understood what was going on within me as I stood inside the store, I simply gave "her" assurance and comfort. I could practically see myself holding "her" close to my side, as I told "her" that she had nothing to fear. I was grown up now, and I could protect "her"; she didn't have to run anymore.

Even now, sharing this memory with you evokes tears as I think about the insight and healing I experienced that day.

Honesty and acceptance of ourselves is so pivotal to our peace and wholeness. We must be able to face what and who we are within.

Those who have the courage to do so find the experience absolutely liberating, and with that liberation comes a new found ability to see people differently.

To accomplish this, you must ask questions of yourself. When you react or are affected in negative ways, you need to find out why.

People have experiences similar to the one I had in the store all the time. They may be left feeling suddenly annoyed, intimidated or depressed. But they are so out of tune with themselves that they have no idea why. They just go with it instead of growing from it.

For example, I knew of a woman who would become terribly upset if someone ate the last portion of her food without letting her know. Most would probably feel disappointed or annoyed given the same situation. However, what my friend experienced was far beyond that.

Being one who believed in self-analysis, she struggled with how the circumstances affected her. Finally, she realized that her intense reaction was due to the lack of food she experienced as a child.

She had lived through the Great Depression, when food for many families was very scarce. As an adult she was extremely careful not to run out of anything. She would experience immense anger when she ran out due to someone else's negligence. The child within her who lived too long with the fear of running out of food found it unacceptable.

The point is feelings, reactions or impulses are evoked all the time as a result of past, unresolved experiences. Regretfully, most of us dash through our lives so quickly, dismissing their effects, and thus throwing away the keys to a less stressful and healthier way of life.

Getting to know oneself is a process. It takes the same motivation and interest as one would have in getting to know a potential soul mate.

However, as you plug into this process, you must believe, no matter what you discover regarding yourself, when there's time enough for growth, it doesn't matter what you've done, only what you will do.

When possible, learn to know those family members or individuals who influenced your life. Gain knowledge and understanding regarding their past and the events that molded their lives. By doing so, you will find it easier to forgive and care for them, as you gain greater insight into all that you are.

## WHEN YOUR SPOUSE GETS ON YOUR NERVES

The relationship between a husband and wife is a delicate subject. Unlike our biological family members, a spouse is an individual that we actually chose to make a part of our family. As such, most bring children into this world, and the experiences we share as a new family unit will contribute—be it for better or for worse—to what and who we are.

Therefore, how much you can actually tolerate the flaws, faults and annoying habits of a potential spouse should be given great consideration before making a commitment to spending the rest of your life with that person. However, due to circumstances that we permit to misguide our reason and choices, things are often not what they should be. Many times we don't give ourselves enough time to get a good look inside of the people we marry, or to get to know those who have influenced their lives.

Nevertheless, it is a choice we make. Hence, it does not take a rocket scientist to figure out how such a choice could turn one's world upside down, if made in haste or without guidance and wisdom.

Furthermore, I dare say, that no one, while considering the wrong person to marry, was able to do so without warning, in one form or another.

I share all of the above, primarily, for those who have not yet made their choice.

Still, for those who may be living with a spouse who is a constant source of vexation, I admonish you to review and apply the recommendations given in Chapter Three (3) under the sub-headings titled: "Co-workers" and "Ducks & Eagles."

When reviewing the above reference, pay close attention to the portions that speak of self-examination. In many cases, if one person in a marriage is willing to do what's good and right for the relationship, the other one will follow — or leave.

I believe in adhering to what the Bible teaches when it comes to the subject of divorce, or any subject for that matter. However, I also believe in THE ALMIGHTY's ability to give those who belong to HIM an escape when faced with more than they can bear.

In other words, if you are doing all that you can do to apply Caring Concern and everything else a marriage requires, THE ALMIGHTY can handle an unyielding spouse without you having to do anything that would affect your relationship with HIM.

On the other hand, if you knew better but married the wrong person anyway and are now suffering the consequences, I believe that's what's referred to as "reaping what you've sown."

If that is the case, you could take matters into your own hands and make an even bigger mess of your life. Or, you could determine to do things THE ALMIGHTY's way, endure your consequences and beseech HIM, through The Christ, to help you straighten out the mess you're in.

As for non-believes, or those who may believe but have not given THE ALMIGHTY rule in their lives, all I can say is, you're on your own.

One of the disadvantages of living a life where you depend solely on you as your everything is that you **can** put more on you than you can bear. Furthermore, without THE ALMIGHTY'S intervention, you may not be able to get yourself out from under your self-made burdens.

I don't mean to get preachy here, but you must understand, I view a relation with the founder of life not as religion but as necessity. You have only to consider the above scenario to figure out why.

Also consider that the very institution we are referring to was established by that same entity.

Therefore, if you have entered into this institution without belief in its founder, well, color me crazy, but based on my belief system, that's just not a wise way to go. In any case, I really don't know what to tell you without interjecting what HE has to say.

This is why I made it absolutely clear in the beginning that this guide is based on HIS WORD and Wisdom.

Building or accomplishing anything together with another human being is a challenge because you have two separate individuals, each with his or her own inner households, attempting to reach one goal. But the rewards that come from successfully building a life together with the one you love are absolutely amazing.

*As it was written: Your enemies
shall be of your own household.*

# NOTES

# Chapter 5

## Put Out!

UP TO THIS point, our focus has been what we can change about ourselves, the things we can do in order to reduce or eliminate the effects that others may have on our nervous systems.

After all, we don't have control over those outside of ourselves.

In fact, generally speaking, as human beings, there's really very little we do have control over. Recognizing that fact is a rude awakening for many, but it's true nonetheless.

Think about it. We don't have control over the condition of the food or water we consume. We basically trust that what we buy from stores won't kill us. We don't have control over the condition of the air we breathe. If a contaminant were released that could wipe us out in a matter of minutes, there would be absolutely nothing we could do about it.

The list goes on and on.

Many times, we tend to think that we can change someone. But the fact is no one can enable another human being to change anything they don't wish to change. Furthermore, they need to want change for themselves far more than you do.

Learn from the founder of human life.

Though HE may intervene and come close enough to influence one's choice, the effect is only temporary if it was not a choice one would make on one's own.

Though HE may give human beings all the power they need to change, it will be of no avail if they choose not to put it to use.

If an individual makes the choice to accept your help and guidance, that's GREAT!

But it has to be his or her choice.

For seven years I ran a non-profit organization, now known as Teens Express.  In fact, I still serve as its President. Our programs are geared to teaching youth powerful decision-making and other life skills through the arts.

At the end of each program we would recite the following:

## THE WAY I THINK
## DETERMINES MY CHOICES AND DECISIONS,
## AND MY CHOICES AND DECISIONS
## DETERMINE THE QUALITY OF MY LIFE!

It's a powerful statement and absolutely true.

So hopefully by now, if you had any doubts before, this guide has successfully convinced you to keep your control switch set on YOU.

But, what do you do about individuals who make lousy decisions that affect their lives and yours? What do you do with someone who claims to be your friend, while proving over and over again that he or she is not trustworthy?

What about relatives who are always taking, yet unwilling to give or do for themselves?

The answer?  Two words: PUT OUT!

As an adult capable of taking care of yourself, you have a choice as to who is permitted to be a part of your life.

I mean, other than the human beings that we bring into this world—and that's only up to a certain age or point—it's up to you who will or will not have access into your life.

Let me define what I mean by "part of your life" by first explaining what I do not mean.  I do not mean that you should disregard, ignore or mistreat anyone.  I do not mean you should reject any necessity or assistance, justly needed, by another human being.

Now, let me give you an example of what I do mean.

I have someone I am related to, whom I truly love and care about.

However, due to years of consistent discord, I could no longer permit this person to be a part of my life.

Therefore, I do not call, unless it's absolutely necessary. We don't go out or socialize, nor do we request anything from each other.

In essence, I do not expose (make vulnerable) myself or my life to this individual. This was not always the case. For years, I did everything within my power to work out the differences.

But soon it became painfully apparent that the conflicts could not be truthfully resolved. Thus, an active involvement in each other's lives would continue to cause undue stress and consternation.

After accepting this, I was done. I made sure that he understood that I loved and cared about him and always would. But, for the sake of peace—which I must have within my life—I had to let go and put him out of it.

However, even now, if he had a need and no one else to turn to, he knows I would do whatever I could to help him. Based on my belief system alone, I would feel compelled to treat him like any other human being (i.e., my neighbor).

The operative words here are "whatever I could do." When it comes to what I do for others, the difference between me and most is I strive not to make choices based on sentiment.

Sentiment is simply thinking with your feelings. It can persuade a mother to shelter and lie for her son, even though he's a fugitive. It can pressure a sister to loan her brother money again and again, even though he's never paid her back a dime from countless other loans.

Sentiment will move a daughter to give her mother sugar laden candy, even though she's a diabetic.

Sentiment can ruin lives, even kill, unintentionally of course.

One must be careful never to confuse sentiment with com-passion. Compassion is when we're compelled to do something **good or beneficial** because of an obvious need.

But sentiment does not consider facts or consequences. It is decision-making based on how one is feeling at the time.

By making choices or decisions void of sentiment, I can discern, with guidance from THE ALMIGHTY, if it truly is a need and, if not, what the true need may be.

Yet to many, a choice void of sentiment might be looked upon as heartless or cold.

Tough love is so often frowned upon in our country. That's because Americans are so nice. In fact, generally speaking, we may be some of the most pleasant, polite and courteous people on the planet, which may explain why we also have one of the highest percentages of citizens with high blood pressure, kidney failure, depression and obesity.

Oh and what do you know, all of these conditions can easily stem from an unhealthy emotional foundation.

I said it once, and I'll say it again and again: We cannot grow on lies, especially when they come in the form of smiles expressing one thing while we think another.

## HOW SENTIMENTAL ARE YOU?

Here's a quick test you can take to help determine if you are sentimental.

Scenario: There is a woman in your life that you have a close (non-romantic) relationship with.

Throughout the years in which you've known her, she has managed to eat herself to the point of disability.

Now, unable to work or effectively do for herself, she frequently looks to you for money. She solicits you often for help with financial obligations and medication, some of which she could do without if she would simply lose the weight.

## Questions:

1) **Would you give her the money? If so, how often?**
2) **If not, is there anything you would do to help her?**

Think about your answers, then stop here. Do not read past this sentence until after you've written down your answers.

Have you written them down? Don't cheat!

Ok, next question:

What if the woman was your mother?

Are you now inclined to change your answer? If so, be absolutely honest as you ask yourself the next question.

**Why would you now consider changing your answer?**

If the only answer you can come up with is "because she's my mother," then your influence is sentiment. It certainly is not what would be best for your mother.

It doesn't matter if it's your mother, father, sibling, spouse or child. If you want to show true Caring Concern for someone, you have to discern what would serve his or her highest good.

That's what THE ALMIGHTY does. HE gives according to what HE knows is right, good and edifying. As for what we ask HIM for, HIS children are supposed to learn from HIM and make requests according to what HE's taught them.

Any good parent would do the same. Why? Because they want what's best for their child.

Should our natural children be the only human beings we share that type of concern for?

Abraham Lincoln once said, "The worst thing you can do for those you love is the things they could do for themselves."

Now I didn't know Abe personally, but based on what I do know about him, I think he's a pretty credible guy to listen to regarding this subject. Especially since historians tell us that he believed strongly in being honest.

In fact, he also said, "I always tell the truth because that way I don't have to remember what I said." It earned him the nickname "Honest Abe."

So many times we hurt the ones we claim to love the most due to sentiment. Sentiment blinds us to what the real need is. Only when we look at a situation void of sentiment can we see clearly what's best for the individual.

I know of a dad who permitted his daughter to come live with him. He complained to me about how the daughter did not wish to clean, or work, or contribute to the bills. Too often he would find himself fussing about it. He shared with me how bad it made him feel, but that he had to do it in order to get through to her.

The fact was he wasn't getting through to her. No matter how upset he became or how much he raised his voice, she continued to do—or in this case, not do—what he requested of her as a resident in his home.

His daughter was a young woman in her early twenties. So when he told me that he didn't wish to fuss at her, I asked him why did he, especially since it wasn't doing any good? We were not talking about a minor child; we were talking about a grown woman.

If he wanted to truly help his daughter, he needed to give her an ultimatum and a set time to meet it.

Either do what you need to do in order to stay or find some place else to live.

Since his daughter was lazy, not stupid, she would more than likely make the necessary changes unless she had some place else to go. If that was the case, hey, problem solved.

Unless, of course, the father had other motives for putting a roof over her head, such as loneliness or guilt due to missed opportunities during her childhood. We will discuss the pit falls that can result from that type of thinking later.

For now, let's get back to the obvious.

By raising his voice and telling his daughter the same things over and over again, he was doing himself and his daughter a great injustice. Who doesn't know how frustrating and stressful it is to talk, yell or nag at someone to do what they should have the common sense, or thoughtfulness, to do on their own?

Most of the time, the talking is hurting both of you. There's a time for talking, and there's a time for walking.

The removal of sentiment can enable us to make wiser choices for others and ourselves. Many battered spouses permit themselves to stay subject to physical abuse due to sentiment.

Permitting ourselves to be taken in by a sob story, tears or the dreaded "pleeeeeeeassse" is not a show of true Caring Concern, but pure sentiment.

Rid yourself of sentiment, and your life will become a lot less stressful. Your choices will also become more beneficial for you and others.

Prayerfully and carefully examine your life. See if there is anyone or anything in it you need to put out. By doing so you would not only help the person or persons, you would also help yourself to a more productive and peaceful life.

If you come to the conclusion that there is a need to PUT OUT, then discern the best way to handle the circumstances and proceed accordingly.

Don't let sentiment get in your way.

*Wherefore, seeing we are compassed about by so great a cloud of witnesses, let us lay aside every burden that hinders us and the old habits that can so easily discomfort us, and let us run with endurance the race that is set before us, looking to the Christ as the author and finisher of our belief; who for the joy that was set before Him endured the tree ("cross"), despised the shame, but is now sitting at the right hand of His FATHER, THE SOVEREIGN.*

*Yea, think on Him who endured such contradictions of transgressors who were against Him, lest you become weary and give up your fight, for you have not yet resisted to the shedding of your blood, striving against transgressors.*

# NOTES

# Chapter 6

## When You Just Don't Feel Like It

FACE IT: some of us are just moody. Sometimes we feel like dealing with people, and sometimes we don't.

Moodiness is a subject I know a lot about. In fact, if you look in the dictionary under the word moody, you might find pictures from my family album.

But moodiness is the least of my family's problems. For there were, and still are, members of my biological family with a tendency to be just plain mean. I'm talking MEAN!

I recall a time when I caught my grandfather yelling outside to someone through his bedroom window. He was not aware that I was listening, though I'm not sure it would have mattered.

He was threatening to come outside to beat up somebody if he ever caught that person walking a dog on his lawn again.

I assumed he was yelling at one of the children in the neighborhood. Was I surprised or amazed that my grandfather would threaten to beat up someone else's child? Based on what I knew about my granddad, I have to say, no, I'm afraid not. However, I was curious to know which child, so I ran to his bedroom window immediately after he left, but the only person I saw walking a dog was an old woman. Now that still amazes me to this day.

Yet, this example is mild compared to some of the things I've seen and heard from certain members of my family while growing up.

I share this with you because there have been times when I was aware of the presence of this "Mean Gene" within me. There have been times when I felt so moody and irritable that the temptation to make miserable anyone who came within my path was almost overwhelming.

The more I grew spiritually and the closer my relationship with THE ALMIGHTY grew, the better I became at fighting against that feeling by simply not giving in to it. But still, when it would come over me, (because of my beliefs) I would wonder if others could see that it was in me.

I can't begin to convey how long and how much I struggled with the fact that I could even experience those types of feelings.

What a relief and how liberating it was to finally learn that it's not what I feel that I need to be concerned about, it's why and what I do while experiencing it.

## FEELINGS COME & GO

*Feelings Come & Go* is actually the title of an e-book that can be found and downloaded, from freshviewbooks.com. The e-book was the result of a workshop I provided during the 90s, also titled *Feelings Come & Go*.

I throw in this commercial because the e-book in conjunction with the content of this guide could be extremely beneficial.

Now, back to our program:

So many times we hear or read that we should control our feelings. For example, we are told to "control our anger." This statement is misleading without clarification of what the speaker or writer actually meant.

I believe clarification of whether we can or cannot control our feelings is extremely important, especially if we are to live and work successfully among those with challenging characters or personalities.

Non-physical feelings, such as anger or fear, work a lot like our physical feelings.

Could you hold a golf ball (for example) in the palm of your bare hand without feeling it? Well, unless your hand is severely damaged, the answer to that question would have to be "No."

Even blindfolded, you would experience, physically, a feeling that would indicate that an object had been placed in the palm of your hand.

You would also, more than likely, be able to tell that the object you were holding was a golf ball. That is, if you had ever held a golf ball. For then, although blindfolded, you would be able to draw the information you needed to identify the object from the information already stored in your memory bank.

The point is, as in the case of the golf ball, we cannot hold on to certain thoughts or ways of thinking without having certain feelings evoked.

However, just as a severely damaged hand might not feel the golf ball, we know there are some individuals whose thinking is so severely damaged, they don't experience feelings in the same manner as most. But that's the exception to the rule.

The rule is: If we entertain certain thoughts, certain feelings may come as a result of those thoughts. Feelings are indicators. Therefore, feelings are going to come, or go, based on what or how we think.

That's what feelings do. Part of their job is to indicate how our thoughts are affecting us, and we have no control over that process.

This information was of great relief to me and maybe to others who have a tendency to feel upset because they feel upset.

So many times, we feel bad for feeling a certain way. When we do that, it's like getting upset with the fire alarm because there's a fire! What we feel is not the problem.

The feelings we experience can be used to direct our attention to where the real problem lies, i.e., what or how we're thinking at the time.

Therefore, I don't believe it's our feelings we control.

However, once feelings come, I do believe that we can and should control how we react to those feelings or what we do while experiencing them. That may be what's implied by the phrase "Control your anger."

We can control the way we react to feelings simply by controlling what or how we think. I said it was simple, not easy, which is probably why so many neglect to do it.

Nonetheless, here's where suppression can be used in a positive way.

If you really think about it, you can very easily come to the conclusion that our ability to think controls just about everything.

The book you're now holding was first a thought before it became a physical reality. The same is true of the chair or couch you may be sitting on and everything else you see around you.

Everything we say or do, every choice or decision we make, is a result of how or what we think. The same also applies to how we experience life. However, though our thoughts control a vast portion of our lives, what or how we think does not control, change or negate the truth (i.e., reality).

Accepting this fact, regarding our thoughts and reality, is an absolute prerequisite for anyone endeavoring to live in peace with others and improve the quality of their lives overall.

However, there are far too many who do not accept this fact. Instead, they develop the habit of devising excuses or false justifications that will permit them to do whatever they <u>feel like doing</u>.

Oh but when those feelings pass, as feelings always do, they're often left facing devastating consequences, even worse, their lives — wasted.

Feelings are temporary impulses. Life and people are so much more important than these fleeting urges we experience.

When you experience a feeling that makes you uncomfortable, take the time to ask yourself where the feeling came from. You may be surprised at the answer.

The joy and freedom that can result from applying the principles found in this guide cannot be realized by anyone who is comfortable being a slave to their impulses or feelings.

You do not have to subject yourself to what you may feel at any given time or moment. So if you are one who is not comfortable living your life that way, this guide, together with the natural abilities you've been given and the power available from THE ALMIGHTY through HIS Son, can enable you to change.

Your relationship with others, and yourself, depends on it.

*To not have knowledge of what you're feeling is not good; and whoever acts in haste is in danger of transgression.*

# NOTES

# Chapter 7

## Digging In

## IDEALISM OR REALITY?

THIS PORTION OF this chapter is for those who may read this guide and think, "This is all based on idealism." Or those who might think, "This stuff just won't work in the real world."

To those people, I say, "How sad." How sad that the thought of taking out the time to care for other human beings would be considered idealistic.

How sad that we live in a world exposed daily to the type of media that depicts Caring Concern as idealistic and bang 'um up, rip 'em off as reality.

Yes, there is evil in the world and a lot of it. But evil works through people. Therefore, if people would stop accepting evil as normal and goodness as idealistic, maybe we could actually change things.

All we have to do is focus on truly caring for one another. We need to discern what's right to do, especially when it comes to our children.

If we did that enough, then perhaps we would raise fewer individuals who are so hurt, angry and emotionally damaged that they wish to take it out on the world by perpetrating massacres within schools or as serial killers.

I watch and applaud programs such as Oprah's and others that endeavor to inspire humans to do their part.

However, there may be those who feel a little deflated when they see the phenomenal things others are doing.

They may find themselves thinking, "I can't do that or anything like that. I can barely do for me. What difference can I truly make in this world?"

Well, you're holding the answer in your hand. This guide shows you how you can make a difference in your life and the lives of others. All you have to do is take the time to care.

If you can help one person to feel better about who they are as a human being due to the attention or treatment you gave that individual, you made a difference. You changed a life.

Consider how many lives we could affect, positively, if we were to apply these principles just some of the time. Better yet, what if we were to apply them most of the time?

PARENTS, what power you posses! If all parents would get their heads out of their concerns for their own needs and focus on the needs of their children, what a difference it would make.

Human beings, for the most part, become what they become as a result of their childhood experiences. Parents, you control a great degree of those experiences.

Yet there are parents who don't know how to be parents. There is no longer an excuse for that. Regardless of age or circumstances, if you live in America, there are books, support centers (online and off), programs and other parents that you can seek out to gain the knowledge you need.

You have one of the most important jobs in the world, and it requires training. If a human being is in this world due to a choice you made, you have a job to do. It's a big job; it's an awesome job!

But, if you do it well, in my opinion, you have contributed to this world something that neither power nor money could buy.

I stated in the beginning: "If you believe in a power greater than yourself and have a longing to live your life to the fullest, free from the unnecessary stress generated by this crazy world we live in, this book is definitely for you."

I also made it clear that I am one who believes in the power of THE ALMIGHTY.

Therefore, the principles in this book are based on what HE expects of us when it comes to our dealings with one another as human beings or neighbors.

Believe it or not, any good that humans possess is due to the character and essence of their Designer.

This is why it's often said that there is good in all human beings. In other words—for those of you who believe in creation—the Creator was first. The Creator is good. The Creator designed humans. Therefore, what good exists in the world is largely due to the good in humans, but both good and humans originated from the Creator.

Now, one might ask, "So where did evil originate?" The word "**Evil**," according to Reader's Digest Dictionary, means: "Causing injury, damage, or any other undesirable result; harmful or prejudicial."

Based on that definition and what knowledge I have of HIS WORD, I believe that evil is anything or any entity that opposes the Creator. It was originated by the first to oppose HIM, and I think we all know who that was.

But have no doubt, THE ALMIGHTY is still just that—All Mighty. HE is still, and will always be, large and in charge.

Know also, if you will accept it, that HE has not changed. The same power HE used to enable HIS Son to rise again after the death of His body is the same power anyone has access to who longs to live life HIS way.

So please, don't accept the current condition of this world as normal. It is not! It's become nonsensical. It's far from normal; if anything it's abnormal.

What we so willingly accept as reality exists because of the thoughts, choices and actions of human beings and the powerful influences behind them. The physical world we know is made up of human beings. Therefore, we make it whatever it is and whatever it will be by the choices we make as individuals.

Do what you've always done, and you'll always get the same results.

If you're tired of the same results, you now have knowledge you can apply on a day-to-day basis. Use it, and it will change your life and the lives of those around you.

If you wish to, you can make that your reality.

Other than within this paragraph, you will not find the phrase **"it's easy"** mentioned in this entire book.

The principles taught in this guide are not easy. It's a growing process for which each day provides opportunities to apply what you've learned.

However, as the process evolves, our lives grow more peaceful. Things that once disturbed us cease to have the same effect. Life begins to look different.

Yes, you will have times or moments when you will find yourself doing as you've done in the past, giving into feelings or thoughtlessness. Don't let the mistakes or stumbles thwart or permanently defeat you.

I end this portion of the chapter with a phase that I have striven to live by, as I focus on using my life for HIS purpose:

*"If I Have The Longing,*
*HE Has The Power.*
*Therefore, It Can Be Done."*

## PUTTING ON & PUTTING OFF

Assuming that you have accepted the challenges presented within the pages you've already read, I would like to focus now on various practices or steps that can help one apply the principles found within this guide.

We often hear the phrase "you have to break that habit." However, habits are not broken; they are replaced.

When it comes to how we are affected or affect people, we must change the manner in which we think. Just as with any habit, one has to replace one way of thinking with another. Eventually, through practice, the old is replaced by the new.

This is referred to as "Putting on and Putting off."

For example:

If you are in the habit of paying no attention to the people around you and you wish to change, you simply put off not paying attention and make a conscious effort to notice people.

What if you are in the habit of pre-judging or being overly critical of other human beings? Then, you must put off thinking that you are in a position to judge others unrighteously and put on focusing on your own faults.

You do this by making a conscious effort to pay attention whenever you are pre-judging or being critical. If you truly wish to replace this habit, you will begin to feel very uncomfortable whenever you fall into it.

Once you have your own attention, you can ask yourself, with each judgmental or critical thought, "What about me, what about the things I need to change?"

However, when dealing with a fault such as being too judgmental, it's good to first examine yourself and discern why you developed the habit in the first place.

It's important to note a very key word when considering the above suggestions. That word is "conscious." You must make a "conscious effort." This is important to note because this is where most fail in replacing old habits.

Remember when you first learned to drive? In the beginning you had to make a conscious effort to remember where everything was, how to do this, then that.

However, the more you practiced your driving, the less you had to consciously (i.e., with awareness) think about everything you had to do while driving. But first you had to put off walking, asking someone else for a ride or using public transportation, by putting on getting behind the wheel of a car.

Eventually the new practice became habit.

A habit is basically something you have practiced long enough to continue doing without concentration or conscious thought.

According to neurological experts, there is a process that takes place within the brain when developing habits.

The brain is made up of cells called neurons. These neurons serve as tiny transmitters with long antennas or branchlike projections called axons. Axons send messages to shorter antennas, called dendrites, which receive them.

These antennas pass the information across tiny gaps called the synapse, from one neuron to the other. The transmissions are electrical in nature.

When the same message goes through this process often enough, deep canyons like grooves are formed, called neural pathways, and a habit is born.

So, neurologically speaking, a habit is actually an imprint formed in the brain that enables you to think, act or feel without the need to consciously think or concentrate.

The more satisfaction or reward we derive from a habit, the more often we repeat it and the deeper the groove becomes. Eventually, the habit is so embedded it becomes extremely difficult to replace.

Therefore, the only way anyone can develop a new habit or replace an old one is to want it very badly.

Years ago, I began snacking or eating a meal whenever I sat down to watch a favorite television program. As she watched how I began to do this on a regular basis, my mentor warned me that I was developing a habit.

Well, even back then I was striving to walk the strait and narrow. I didn't smoke or drink or fornicate, etc. So I thought, what was wrong with it? It wasn't a bad habit.

To me it was such a small thing, and it brought me pleasure, give me a break!

But she, as usual, saw way down the road at what the consequences could be. And, as usual, she was right.

Fifteen years and twenty pounds later, I rued the day I began to develop that habit. It became very hard to just sit and enjoy a TV program unless I was eating or snacking on something.

Endeavoring to replace that habit was almost like going through drug withdrawal.

However, when I got tired enough of seeing those extra pounds in the mirror, I determined that I had to check myself in to my own internal rehab center.

I have yet to check out.

My point is applying the principles within this guide will in fact change the manner in which others affect you. You will begin to see and feel toward others differently.

You will be able to live a more joyful and less stressful way of life. The question is will you apply the principles and how badly do you want the above.

Do you want it badly enough to go through your own internal rehabilitation? Or will you simply continue to think and do as you've always done because it's easier?

Easier, it may be, but what in this life, and the next, are you depriving yourself of in order to stay within your comfort zone?

After all, you chose to read this book. Therefore, you must be looking for answers.

So many times we talk of what we want, what we're tired of or what's wrong in our lives. Many of us go as far as to pray for answers or for change.

We will even accept the answers, provided they don't require much effort or discomfort on our part.

Heaven forbid that we have to actually come out of our comfort zones or give up anything.

Just the other day, I was sharing with my husband the fact that consumers and voters control the United States.

It's true. Think about it. How many violent films or video games do you think manufacturers would produce if only a handful of consumers bought them?

Politicians are **voted** into office in this country.

When African Americans got tired of how they were being treated when using public transportation, they banded together. They determined not to use that system until things changed, even if it meant walking for miles every day.

Once the transit system saw how the Black consumer's dollar affected their bottom line, changes were made.

Consumers and voters determine the state of this country!

However, we relinquish our power because we don't wish to make the sacrifices necessary to exert it. The same principle applies when it comes to doing what's right to and for one another.

And so, I ask again, how badly do you want it? Did you pick up this book because of the title or the funny pictures on the cover? Or does it make you feel better about yourself to talk about all the self-improvement books you read?

How badly do you wish to control the way you're affected by others and the way others are affected by you?

Think about it.

## ROAD RAGE

When it comes to road rage what we're really dealing with is frustration. Frustration is the feeling we experience when we feel hindered and it is nearly always accompanied by anger. I have struggled with the effects of frustration for as long as I can remember. I have prayed, cried and agonized over the manner in which I find myself reacting when frustrated. Therefore I am more than pleased to share the light I received in answer to my desperate longing for power over the effects of this particular source of aggravation.

One of the practices that I continue to develop is the ability to consider the benefits of being delayed. This way of thinking is especially helpful when dealing with road rage. In other words, when you find yourself feeling frustrated because of a driver or traffic, think about how the delay may be saving your life.

I recall endeavoring to get out of the house in order to make an appointment by a certain time, only to encounter one delay after another. By the time I got on the road, I was anxious — which is never a good thing — and rushing to get to my appointment. As I drove to my destination I saw the remains of a terrible accident. For the first time I found myself wondering if all the delays were to ensure that I would avoid that accident.

Perhaps if I had left when I intended to, I would have been one of the drivers in what appeared to have been a devastating collision.

After receiving that insight I endeavored to apply this new way of thinking whenever I found myself hindered due to circumstances beyond my control.

The other challenge many face when frustrated is the tendency to take it out on others, especially those whom we believe responsible for the hindrance. This can be very destructive, especially when dealing with children. What has helped me immensely is admission. Admitting or sharing how we feel enables us to release some of the energy generated by strong feelings or emotions. It's the same relief we experience when we confess to something we've hidden for years. Even when the confession comes with certain consequences, there is still a degree of relief that occurs with admission. Simply let others who are involved know that you don't wish to be unkind or sound harsh, but that you are feeling very frustrated and ask that they bear with you while you deal with it. The children in your life can also learn from your example when you apply this practice, since children often experience frustration due to helplessness.

## TRY A LITTLE HUMBLENESS

A little humility can go a long way. Too often, pride gets in the way of our ability to care for one another. Pride, according to THE ALMIGHTY, is a dangerous, destructive thing. It causes one to think beyond who or what they are or what they're capable of doing.

Pride could make a mouse believe it can whip a lion. But unless THE ALMIGHTY has given the mouse a clear sign that it can rely on more than its own abilities, Mr. Mouse could end up as an appetizer with that attitude.

Sometimes the ability to simply say "I am sorry" or "I was wrong" can open vistas.  Yet humbling oneself to say and mean those words is extremely difficult for most.

In fact, some go to ridiculous extremes to avoid it.

Men especially seem to think standing on their pride (not principles) makes them strong and powerful.

When in fact, humility has far more power than pride.

Think about it.   Which would you submit to: a person standing in front of you telling you — with words or attitude — what you will do because they said so, or one who would humbly ask what they want of you?

If the goal is to gain your consent, most would be inclined to submit to the humble request.

The old cliché "you can catch more flies with sugar than with vinegar" is generally true.

Hey, if humility can move THE ALMIGHTY from wrath to mercy, I'm thinking it's powerful stuff.

Yet most feel to show humility would make them weak or a doormat or less than who they are.  But the truth of the matter is it's quite liberating when you can resist pretending to be something that you're not — especially when it's you who you're endeavoring to fool.

Sometimes, people are turned off at the thought of humility due to the total disregard they were shown during their humble endeavors.

If this describes you, please don't harden yourself and put off developing one of the greatest virtues one can acquire.

Put on humility, and if someone should disregard it, then think about The Christ.  Let your mind go to what He endured at the hands of Pilate's soldiers, who took Him aside and slapped Him around while making fun of Him.  This they did to the Son and heir of HIS HOLY MAJESTY, the only human being who had never let THE ALMIGHTY down, and yet He said and did nothing.

If you are a believer, thinking about that alone should help you.  After all, the word Christian does mean "Like The Christ."

Another antidote would be to think of how pitiful and/or weak the human being showing you the disregard must be. Also, be assured that you are in a far better position and stronger for not permitting yourself to fall where they are.

As for those working with the public or in any position where you might encounter an irate customer or client, I have come up with words one can say that would immediately cause the other individual to clam down. And, it generally works no matter what the situation.

Simply say:

"I regret that you feel that way. I did not intend to offend you in any way."

You can also add to that—when appropriate—"What can I do?"

The key to successfully using the above is to use it only after the person is done complaining, ranting or saying whatever they have to say.

I first came up with this approach as an antidote for those occasions when I know that I am not in the wrong or that the person I am dealing with is definitely at fault, but it's just not appropriate or would do no good to belabor the point. In saying the above, I am admitting to no wrong and letting them know that regardless of what they might **think** I did, it was not my intention to upset them.

PLEASE NOTE: It must be said in love or Caring Concern for the other person. This will not work if you say it with a bad attitude.

If you find yourself tempted to plead your case, keep in mind that it is extremely difficult, if not impossible, to reason with someone when they're upset. Therefore, when you humble yourself instead of becoming defensive, it actually causes the other person to experience a sense of conviction regarding what they've done or said. This is why you let them finish. By permitting them to talk long enough—without your inter-vention—they will have plenty to reflect on later. Not to mention how foolish it feels to argue by yourself.

But of course, it takes one's ability to care enough for the other person, and the willingness to humble oneself, to use this approach.

When dealing with relatives, co-workers or friends, you only need to look at them and then quietly say: "I care about you" and just leave it at that. Just walk away afterwards. You will be amazed at how thought provoking those words will be for the other person, especially if they've just finished making an absolute Butt-Butt of themselves.

A genuine show of humility can change lives. I can also assure you that anyone who focuses on developing it does not have many problems with people getting on their nerves.

*You must put off old habits and former ways of thinking, which are corrupt because of former deceits and lusts. You must be renewed in your thinking and ways. You must put on new ways of thinking, and form new habits, which THE SOVEREIGN approves, which leads to righteousness and true holiness.*

# NOTES

# After Thoughts & Vital Points

IN CLOSING, I would like to revisit certain vital points mentioned in earlier chapters.

In Chapter II: **"When People Get on Your Nerves In General,"** the following questions where addressed:

1) What is the "right" thing to do?
2) In what way am I supposed to treat someone who is nasty or vile?
3) How am I supposed to be towards someone who obviously does not care about me?

All three questions cause me to think of a similar dilemma brought to me by my cousin years ago.

She had determined to speak to strangers she met throughout her day. However, to her dismay, many did not return her salutations. She came to me one day sorely disappointed and on the verge of throwing out the whole idea when I asked her why did she decide to do it in the first place.

Her reply conveyed that she thought it was a good and right thing to do. So then I asked, "Then what difference does it make what the response is?"

I also think of another relative who found it very easy to give. It seemed almost spontaneous for her to give whatever she had to offer. In fact, I've often thought perhaps she had the gift of giving.

If so, it was undeveloped. I began to notice how she would often expect a certain something in return.

She also would talk terribly about the recipient if she didn't get what she expected.

Expecting something back might not be so bad if she at least let these people know what they were getting into.

We had a very intense conversation on this subject when she decided to come to me with a complaint about one of her recipients. I simply said, "If you cannot give without expectations, then don't give at all."

In essence, we should do the right thing because it's the right thing, not because of what we think someone else should or might do.

I think that pretty much covers questions two and three.

As for question number one, the right thing **to you** can only be whatever you understand it to be at the time.

We can only do what we've been taught or know.

For example, if you've been taught that the right thing to do is to physically fight whenever someone threatens to hit you, then to you that's the right thing to do.

So, under those circumstances, if you want to do the right thing, though you may feel like running, you would not. Based on what you've been taught, you would stand there and fight. Not because you like to fight, but because you want to do the right thing.

This is one of the reasons why many analysts say that truth is relative.

I, for one, believe that truth is absolute and facts can change; it's what we know that's relative.

Therefore, I don't dare diminish the resolution truth carries. Nor do I argue with facts, if I know for certain that it is indeed a fact.

However, if we do not know the facts or the truth regarding a matter, we can only act on what we do know.

Let's look again at the above example. The fact is if you hit someone based on a threat, you could be charged with assault. As a fact, it has the potential for change. However, as it stands, right now in America it's against the law to physically attack someone regardless of the words they use, which means somebody could talk about your momma, and the most you can do is talk back without the threat of criminal consequences.

But what if you don't know that? What if you are from another country where it's been deeply ingrained in you that you would be wrong and cowardly not to strike under those circumstances?

The answer is you would either strike or suffer a great deal of guilt and shame. That's because based on what you know, to strike would be the right thing to do.

This is why THE ALMIGHTY judges according to one's motives and what they know. It's also why one is without excuse once they receive what they need to know.

You, as a result of reading this guide, may now have extended or greater knowledge of how we, as one human race, should treat one another and the effort that's required to do so.

To simply disregard it or make excuses will never negate the fact that you now know.

That's why the WORD makes clear that it's better to not know than to know and not do.

As for the absolute truth, I have to look to the authority and power of THE ALMIGHTY.

Most refer to HIM as "GOD," as did I. However, when you have a deep appreciation for HIS Almighty Power and Majesty, you may sometimes find yourself feeling a little offended when others use the title "GOD" in a disrespectful way or in connection with profanity or slang. In addition to that, the title, by one definition, can be used pertaining to anyone or anything to which one bows down or gives homage.

So I determined a long time ago, when using a title that pertains to HIM, I would use THE ALMIGHTY or SOVERIGEN instead. I felt confident that they were both titles that only HE is worthy of and could not imagine how others could misuse either of them.

But regardless of what titles HIS children may use, as long as we know that it pleases HIM and is used in reverence and adoration for who and what HE is, I believe HE would find them acceptable and used with earnest.

I also believe that HE is the author of truth and what is truly right or righteous simply comes down to what HE says it is.

However, as pointed out previously, HE knows us. Therefore, HE takes into account the individual circumstances of every human being and determines accordingly.

But I must interject here an instance that will drive home a very important point.

I sat with a pastor of a small assembly (church) one day. He shared with me the fact that he did things he knew were not right or pleasing to THE ALMIGHTY. He went on to say that when the time came to face HIM, he could only hope that HE would have mercy on him.

I looked up at him with a puzzled look on my face as I said, "But HE's doing that now."

Think about who we're discussing here.

This is the same entity that designed the human anatomy. The same entity that brought the Universe into being, including every single thing we mortals use to construct anything we make.

HE has not changed. HIS power has not diminished.

Therefore, HE is able to provide us with whatever we need in order to know and live according to HIS purpose.

So, though HE is longsuffering and will take us where we are, HE does not give us an excuse to stay there, which is just one of the reasons why HE preserved a letter written to disciples long ago in Rome by one of HIS most cherished apostles. It contained the following words:

> *Do you despise the richness of HIS goodness? HIS forbearance and long-suffering? Not being aware that the goodness, forbearance and longsuffering of THE ALMIGHTY SOVEREIGN is to give you time to convert* **(change).**

In Chapter 3, titled **"PUT OUT!"** we looked at an example involving a dad who might have ulterior motives for putting a roof over his daughter's head.

I wish to revisit this point due to how often this occurs between parent and child.

Parents make all sorts of decisions concerning their children that have nothing to do with what's best for the child—now an adult. Loneliness and/or guilt seem to be at the top of the list for motives.

We hear and see through the media the most horrific stories of what parents do to their children. But it's those subtle ways parents negatively affect their children I wish to address.

Some mothers use their children as their own private social/fan club. Some experience jealousy if their children show a special like or favoritism towards another adult. They may even go as far as to manipulate the child into feeling guilty about the other relationship.

Others wish to maintain or exert control over their children, far into their adulthood and want their children to believe that they can.

How many times have you heard someone, perhaps yourself, say to a child: "You're mine!" In other words, "You belong to me."

Our children do not belong to us. When they come into this world, by use of our reproduction systems, we have an awesome responsibility.

Regrettably, many either do not accept the responsibility at all, or they take it to an extreme. These are all areas that I admonish parents to examine carefully when it comes to their own children.

The rights of children is a very sensitive subject for me. I absolutely oppose abused helplessness, especially when it comes to children. They don't ask to come into this world. Yet, too often, they find themselves under adults who care very little about themselves, not to mention a helpless child.

This is just one more reason why the principles found in this guide are so crucial.

If you are a parent who has difficulty caring about yourself, then you can be certain that you are not caring for your child in the manner that he or she deserves.

I challenge you to truly examine yourself and your relationship with your child, based on the principles in this book.

Hopefully, you will be able to see in ways you've never seen before.

Before leaving the issue of parents and their children, I really need to say a word regarding our teenagers.

## PARENTS EVERYWHERE HEAR MY CRY!
### These Young Folks Need Our Help!

So many of them are like walking Zombies. Is it what they're eating? Is it in the water? I mean, what's going on?

I was in a long line at the grocery store. I stood there assuming that it was moving slowly due to a customer either in need of a price check or writing one. But when I leaned over to see what was going on, I saw an older teenage boy, playing one potato two potato with each customer's groceries.

When I finally arrived at the cash register, I looked at his name tag and said, "Ricardo, honey, push a button, pull a string, flip a switch, do something! Should I get you an espresso?"

He looked at me and laughed and then continued—Five-hundred and Four Potato.

Ok, I'm stretching that story, just a bit, but you get my point.

Where is the energy teenagers once had?

AND ANOTHER THING! Have the manufacturers of fashions for youth stopped making clothes that fit? It would seem they are making them too small for the girls and too big for the guys! I really don't know the answers to these questions. My only child ceased being a teenager years ago.

Nevertheless, if you are currently a parent of a teenager and it sounds like I'm describing your child, please find out what's going on and help them out.

Let's keep in mind, if The Christ should tarry, these are the very folks that will be running things in this country in just a few decades. Hopefully, by then, the males will be able to do so without the threat of their pants falling down.

━━━━━━━━━━━━━━━━━

In chapter II, titled "WHEN PEOPLE GET ON YOUR NERVES IN GENERAL," the statement was made: "Sometimes the right solution is the simplest and most obvious one, but the hardest to accept."

With that statement a story about a man with a horse comes to mind. He wanted his horse to be a hard worker. So he consulted ten horse breeders. Nine of the breeders told him, "If you take good care of the horse, it will take good care of you." They then proceeded to tell him all it would entail.

The tenth breeder told him, "Just use a whip anytime the horse doesn't perform."

Though common sense and concern for the animal should have made it absolutely clear that the simple advice of the first nine breeders was the obvious solution, the man accepted the advice of the tenth breeder. Why? Because though it would make it harder for the horse, it was the easiest solution for the man.

In today's world, how often are choices made that result in suffering and even death because the decision makers wish to take the path that requires the least amount of effort, even though there's an obvious and simple solution that could save lives or spare suffering right before them?

Simple does not always mean easy; the two words are not necessarily synonymous. Doing what's right according to THE ALMIGHTY's standards is not easy, especially in today's world.

However, doing what's right is the simplest and often most obvious solution to any situation.

No matter how complicated or technical life appears, when you get right down to basics, it's all very simple.

Truth is also simple. In fact, when it appears to be complicated, you can be certain a lie has slipped in from somewhere.

Things only get complicated when someone makes a mess due to an awful choice or decision.

Faulty choices tend to have a domino effect. To make matters worse, many try to cover them up with criminal choices.

Most bad decisions are made due to fear, greed, lust or power. When any one or more of these motivators are involved, the truth can become completely disabled, losing its ability to intervene.

And there you have it — the world we live in.

On the other hand, when a situation is void of all those things, the truth is free to penetrate and people can actually think harmoniously. You've seen it happen. Groups of people get together, everybody's in agreement, except for the ones with their own agendas.

The solution was simple until Johnny Greed or Joan Fearful intervened.

Life is less stressful when we seek the simple solutions. The world makes more sense when we accept the obvious.

This entire guide is made up of simple solutions. However, it all comes down to seven simple steps:

1.  Make sure that you have accepted and love yourself. This requires you to be honest with yourself and to take the time to know and control your inner household.
2.  Think of every human being as your family member.
3.  Focus on showing Caring Concern by putting yourself aside long enough to see the person in front of you.
4.  When looking at someone, practice seeing the child they once were. This exercise alone will enable you to look

past the barriers and false fronts to the core of an individual.

5. Do not permit yourself to be a slave to sentiment or what you maybe feeling at the moment.

6. Make decisions based on what would serve one's highest good.

7. Plug into the power source that can enable you to become who you were truly meant to be.

Again, I stress that because something is simple does not make it easy. Nothing listed above is easy, but then nothing worthwhile ever is. But you can do it. You can do it all. It only requires one thing:

You must long for it so much that you're willing to do whatever it takes to have it. Without that, THE ALMIGHTY SOVEREIGN HIMSELF would not be able to help you apply the knowledge you've gained from this guide.

So many of us speak of wanting a good, peaceful and joyful life, but few are willing to pay the price.

Yes, a life without unnecessary stress, worry or drama comes with a price.

Even The Christ, when sharing what THE ALMIGHTY had to offer, admonished His disciples to first "Count the Cost."

However, it's such a worthwhile purchase. The benefits far outweigh what we have to give or do to attain it. What's really great — no one can take it away from you.

In fact, it's one of the few things in life you can actually take with you. It was one of the last commandments that The Christ left those who were and would be His disciples. He said:

***This is my law, that you care one for another as I have cared for you.*** [Yehochanan (known by most as **John**) 15:12].

I don't think I need to elaborate on the extent to which The Christ cared for us.

The joy, peace and fulfillment we experience by simply developing Caring Concern for one another are eternal. That's far more than we can say for the time, money or other things we permit to keep us from paying attention to one another.

I was tempted to call this work a beginner's guide because it does not go into as much depth as one may find in other written resources.  However, I believe it can help or assist anyone seeking to grow and develop into a more caring human being with the ability to maintain control from within.  Nevertheless, there is a great deal of literature out there that can introduce you to conventional knowledge and practices.  But, it is my humble opinion that none of it will be of benefit if you have not come to accept the simple truths revealed within the pages of the book you are now holding.

―――――――――――――――――

## What To Do When People Get On Your Nerves.

I came up with that title in the hope that it would draw those who needed this guide as much as I did.

If it didn't turn out to be what you thought it would, I sincerely hope that what you discovered enhances your life and your relationship with every member of your family — The Human Race.

I love you, truly — with caring concern.

In that manner, HIS Holy Concern was made known. Not that we were concerned about HIM, but that HE was concerned about us, and enjoined HIS Son HE began to give His body to death, while it hanged on the tree, that through the death of His body we could be set free from the force of evil.

Now, if THE SOVEREIGN was that concerned about us, we ought to be concerned about one another. Not one of us has gazed upon the face of THE SOVEREIGN at any time, but if we are concerned for one another, THE SOVEREIGN's Enabling Power will remain in us, and HIS Holy Concern will be made complete in us.

# NOTES

For more information about

## Life Guide and Corporate Trainer

MoriEl Randolph

including Books, Seminars and Services

visit

**www.answersofinspiration.com**

or call

301 877-0572

You can also visit

www.freshviewonline.com

## Personal Development Books

## Corporate Training Seminars

## Motivational Workshops

## & Inspirational Audio

For more information about

**The Youth Development & Arts Nonprofit Organization**

TEENS! Express!

including its programs or productions

visit

**www.teensexpress.org**

or call

301 877-0592

www.ingramcontent.com/pod-product-compliance
Lightning Source LLC
La Vergne TN
LVHW011244080426
835509LV00005B/626